THE GRASS IS GREENER

Also by Tom Fort

The Far From Compleat Angler

THE GRASS
IS GREENER

Our Love Affair with the Lawn

TOM FORT

HarperCollins*Publishers*

HarperCollins*Publishers*
77–85 Fulham Palace Road,
Hammersmith, London w6 8jb

www.**fire**and**water**.com

Published by HarperCollins*Publishers* 2000
1 3 5 7 9 8 6 4 2

A catalogue record for this book is
available from the British Library

ISBN 0 00 257064 5

Set in PostScript Linotype New Baskerville
with Scotch Roman Display by
Rowland Phototypesetting Ltd,
Bury St Edmunds, Suffolk

Printed and bound in Great Britain by
Clays Ltd, St Ives plc

To my mother

CONTENTS

ACKNOWLEDGEMENTS   ix

Prelude   1

Part One

In the Beginning   15
Pleasures of the Green   32
Shaven Lawns and Vapid Greens   53
The Moral Lawn   72

Musings from the Shed (1)   87
Albert's Morning March

Part Two

Budding Genius   101
The Budding's Flowering   116
The Glory of the Garden   133
Velvet Robes   148
Greensward and Minimum Bovver   172

Musings from the Shed (2)   195
Lawn Order, Man's Business

Part Three

The Lawnsmen   209
The Mowermen   230
My Sward and Others   248

BIBLIOGRAPHY   269
INDEX   271

ACKNOWLEDGEMENTS

The idea for this book came from a visit to my father-in-law's home, during which I suggested to him – quite wrongly – that his lawn was being sabotaged by moss. His outrage at the notion set me thinking about Englishmen and their grass. I am grateful to him, and to my wife Helen, for that and much else besides.

I would also like to express my thanks to: Pippa Lewis, for her invaluable helping hand; Diana Farley, for letting me make use of the indispensable material in her dissertation 'The Development and Use of the Lawn Mower'; Alan Andrews, Lord Deedes, Tony Hopwood, James Rothery, Denis Burles, Andrew Hall, Michael Duck, Steve Curley and Michael Hardy for entertaining me and giving generously of their time; my friends Jeremy Paxman and Stephen Taylor, for reading some of the manuscript and offering their enthusiastic encouragement; Stephen and Jane Lewis for their hospitality; the staff of the Royal Horticultural Society Library, the Reading University Library, the Museum of English Rural Life and Stroud Museum; Barry Bowerman at St John's College, Oxford, Jack Briggs, Jim Crace, Roger Evans, Keith Wotton, Halla Beloff, Michael Argyle and Duncan Snelling; Lloyds of Letchworth, Ransomes of Ipswich and Atco-Qualcast; and, finally, to Susan Watt of HarperCollins, for her perceptiveness, sympathy and good humour.

PRELUDE

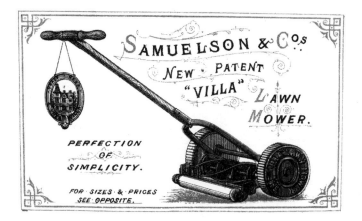

The Lawnsman Cometh

It is mid-April, anywhere in suburban England, any-where among a million courts, crescents, closes, avenues, drives, groves, ways; anywhere the ornamental cherries are in pink flower and the hanging baskets standing guard by the front porch are glowing with spring colour. It is a Saturday. Enough of the morning has gone for breakfast to have been eaten, for the news-paper to have separated into its dozen sections, for the dog to have been tickled behind the ears and the wife brought her tea, for the milk bottles to have been deposited by the step with a dissonant chime; for that breeze, carrying with it the first foretaste of the warmth of summer, to have rid the little kingdom behind the house of the worst of the clammy moisture night has laid on it. Already our man has found time amid his chores to go out and sniff the air. Its savour has brought a softening to his features, a shadow of a smile, while resolv-ing them into an expression of purpose.

I say 'our man', because apart from his maleness and sense of purpose and the fact that he is likely to be between thirty and four score years, I cannot characterize him further. He may be shaven or stubble-chinned, regimentally smart or irredeemably scruffy, self-employed or nine-to-five wage slave, respectably retired, painfully redundant. His demeanour and circumstances tell us nothing. All we may safely say of him is that he cares for the order of the space by his home. We must see him in action.

By now he will, morally, have cleared the decks. He may have walked the dog, made the breakfast, got the paper, tapped the barometer, discharged half a dozen trivial duties; or he may have just rolled out of bed, grabbed a cup of instant and surveyed the scene. In both cases, he will have endeavoured to dispose of clutter. He will have organized himself to be free from distractions. Before his task is done, he will not wish to go to the supermarket or welcome guests. Demands which interfere are likely to make him extremely irritable.

There are preliminaries to the observances. He will dress, not necessarily with care, but properly: perhaps in a boiler suit, or ragged sweater and filthy oil-stained jeans; in what he calls his 'garden shoes', or just grubby trainers. Whatever the outfit, it will be indissolubly associated in his mind with the garden and the duties laid on him by it. With it belong the well-worn gloves, dirt behind the fingernails, the odour of bonfire lingering about the hair, an ache in the lower back, a sudden and virtuous need for tea, that particular expulsion of breath that accompanies a satisfied survey of a job well done.

At ease in the familiar raiment, he makes his way to the shed. To the ignorant observer, this structure will be no more than a utilitarian assembly of wood, brick or breeze block, surmounted by a corrugated roof. More often than not, its condition is decrepit, if not ruinous.

4

But it would be erroneous to deduce deficiency of regard from this neglect. To our man, the shed represents a precious antithesis to the home. It speaks to him of an older, more elemental life. It is a place where he is master, where standards other than those of cleanliness and neatness and newness apply.

To our man, the harsh monosyllable – 'shed' – has a comforting, spiritual resonance. His secular self acknowledges that it is a dumping ground for tools, machinery, teetering towers of old flowerpots, cobweb-festooned stacks of garden chairs with rotted canvas seats, bags of Growmore, packets of ant powder, bottles of weedkiller with tops that will not turn, brushes rigid with ancient creosote, drums of unruly wire netting with last autumn's leaves held crispy in the mesh, loops of wire hanging from rusty nails, saws with rusting teeth which he has intended to oil and clean these past five years, and a great accumulation of other relics.

But to him it is much more than a mere storage space. It is a sanctum, a private place where his soul is nourished. It should have the quiet of a chapel, although in a good cause that may be fractured by electric drill or thumping hammer blows. There is much dust, but it lies still, and the old flies caught in the cobwebs in the corners are undisturbed. The shed is like his mind, crammed with the forgotten, the half-forgotten and the redundant. In its recesses teeter piles of junk, which – if ever retrieved – at once spill their old stories. It is a place to pause, to contemplate, to sniff that rich, musty old smell, to pick up things and put them down again, to arrange and rearrange. It is a place with a force of its own; which he respects, because each time he rolls up his sleeves and becomes extremely dirty imposing order on it, it reverts in its own time to disorder. That is as it should be.

On this morning, our man does not linger among the shadows. He has pressing business with a machine in green. He finds his gloves, slips his hands into their familiar griminess, grasps the well-worn handles, and drags it forth into the sunlight. It may be a modest contraption, requiring no more than a steady push for it to do its work. It may be electric and murmur as it goes, or be powered by petrol, and roar. The motion of its blades may be forward or circular. It may be a foot wide, or four. It may have cost ten pounds at a jumble sale, or three thousand from a showroom. Its common characteristics are its colour – it is, or should be, green – and its function, which is to cut grass.

Although the fundamentals of the ensuing ritual do not vary much, the mood of the devotees does, in a way dictated by the condition of the machine. This has little to do with its cost or quality, but rather the manner in which it was put to rest at the end of the previous mowing season. Broadly speaking, there is a gulf between those who, recognizing that the season is at an end and that another will inevitably come, clean, oil, repair and cover their mowers; and those who do not. I make no moral judgement here, which is as well, for I belong in the second category. It is the case that those in the second category would often wish themselves in the first, while the converse does not apply.

That futile longing is usually at its most intense on this Saturday morning in April. Those who tended properly to their machines when the leaves were tumbling last

November can now regard them with a virtuous smile. The metalwork gleams, the pale tops of the spark plugs wink, the cutters are dark and smooth and sharp (for they have been taken to the workshop in early winter, when they received prompt and unhurried care). This machine is primed and ready.

Contrast this to the shame of us in the second category. We view our machine, not with a self-satisfied smirk, but a grimace of horror. The plug is buried under a clod of slimy, decomposed vegetable matter. There is still grass in the box, mixed with dark, rotted leaves. The cutters are rimmed with accretions of hard earth and fossilized herbage; and, worse, when you scrape this off, you find the cutting edge itself mutilated and split by collisions with stones. You remember: how you swore, but a few months back, that this time you would cherish your loyal servant and attend to its needs; how you finished that last mow as dusk and a dozen competing demands closed in; how you wheeled it, still warm and smoking, into the shed, and abandoned it with your promise; how winter came and the garden became dank, dreary and repulsive, the shed cold and uninviting.

Never mind. It has endured the same each winter and come through. If it had a mind, it would doubtless wish you in the first category as well. But that is a matter of secondary importance, when there is work to be done.

Before operations begin, our man will scout the terrain. Consciously or unconsciously, he will sense that the grass beneath his feet has lost the flabby inertness of its dormancy. There is a spring to it. It is quickening with

7

restored life. Its lustre, the sprouting of the daisies and clover, simultaneously gladden his heart and remind him of his duty. He is most unlikely to stop and ponder why this should be; what it is within him that is fulfilled by the annual taking up of the challenge. He has neither the time nor the inclination to analyse the nature of the drama. There is a lawn to be mowed.

Now, for the first time, we hear the Saturday music of the mower. As sound, it is horrible: loud, discordant, disconnected, structureless. But to those of the faith there is a mysterious sweetness to it. Familiarity annihilates its brutishness, leaving its rhythms, its pauses, its cadences, its crescendos and diminuendos, to exercise their role as indispensable accompaniment to the ritual.

In the case of the push mower and the electric mower, sound and purposeful action come together. But for the petrol-driven mower, there is an overture, initiated by the pulling of the starter rope or cranking of the handle. With first-category devotees, this will be brief: an introductory bar consisting of a couple of smooth pulls, before the rich orchestra of the motor adds its throaty weight. For second-category worshippers, the overture may well be protracted; indeed, it may well be the prelude, not to mowing the lawn at all, but to a hurried dash to the repair shop, a thoroughly unfruitful exchange with an overburdened mechanic, and a day of painful non-consummation.

But this day we will have none of that. The cutters are unclogged, the layers of old muck prized off, the oil checked, the petrol tank filled. The handle is pulled once, twice, three times. The wheel revolves lifelessly. The flow of fuel is checked, the plug cleaned. The rope

8

is yanked in earnest, with a silent prayer that it will not – as has been known – snap in the middle. Now there is, at last, an answering cough, like that of a half-drowned man. It dies, and there are further twiddlings with accelerator and choke. Again the rope is pulled, and this time the music of returning life is heard. Smoke belches, black as impurities are incinerated, then blue. With the depression of the accelerator, the volume increases. The cutters are engaged and the music acquires breadth and depth, as when the tubas and trombones join the orchestra.

For a moment our man is held by the sound, and by the power transmitted from the engine through the handles to his forearms. These forces enclose him, shutting him off from the world of bird song, barking dogs, aeroplanes, his squealing children, a wife who would trouble him with shopping lists or holiday brochures. He grips the handles tight, and guides the machine towards the grass. As he meets the lawn, the cutters engage. The first shower, lush and juicy, shoots forth into the box, emerald spattered with the white of the daisies. But our man's appreciation of the aesthetics is unconscious. His intelligence is focussed on the line he must follow.

The creation of the pattern is central to the ritual. One of the old textbooks recommends that the most pleasing effect is achieved by starting with the outer circumference, and mowing in a continuous, decreasing circuit until the centre is reached and shorn. But that requires what few of us have, a lawn shaped in the shape of a symmetrical oval or circle. Our man observes orthodox practice. He executes two careful circuits of the outer edge to give himself a margin, and once the

9

furthest curve permits, he cuts across it in the first straight lines. As he moves into the main body of the lawn, the lines become longer. It is in the sculpting of those lines that his spirit receives much of its nourishment. Here is rhythm, regularity, the measured tread behind the devouring machine, the sweeping turn at each end as the whizzing blades slice the air within inches of the heads of flowers or the buds of shrubs, before the controlled flourish is completed and it is back to the straight and narrow. And all the time the proportion of the grass which has succumbed to our man's control appreciably and visibly grows, and that left in its quasi-natural state diminishes.

By the time he halts the machine to empty the box for the first time, the comforting familiarity of the ritual has reclaimed him. He may put his nostrils close to the damp mass of cuttings, inhale that fresh, innocent smell which speaks to him of his history as a mower and the lawns he has mown. His pleasure is conscious now, as he marches the old route to his compost heap, lying in mouldering peace in some unregarded corner of his domain, and lays the season's first bright offering over the tea leaves, coffee grinds, potato peel and cabbage stalks. He may pause a moment to spread the cuttings, thinking how many more times he will perform this office before the season of growth is out. Before he is finished this day, that deposit will be buried deep, its greenness yielding to yellow and grey as the bacteria go to work.

Back to his waiting machine our man strides. A quick push or two on the accelerator – whose results are audible half way down the street – and he is off again. See how the beast eats up the ground, while his feet fall with firm, noiseless tread on the beheaded blades. The flower bed looms, but he does not begin the turn until full contiguity with his previous stripe is accomplished. The faded daffodil heads will surely be lost; but no, he sweeps in a circle, tilting back the snarling cutters, easing back on the accelerator, his body following in a disciplined arc. And the next stripe is laid.

Thus, by measurable degree, the task is performed. Somewhere deep inside our man, a need is answered. Were he to be questioned, he would mumble something about having to keep the place tidy. His machine has brought order to the lawn; he orders the machine. A psychologist might identify a different order of precedence among the elements of man, machine and herbage; wondering who or what was really in control, who was whose servant, who whose master; might search deeper still, into the possible symbolism of the stripes, recollections of marks inflicted or suffered in school canings, sublimations of flagellistic or masochistic urges. Our man's need might be inadequacy, his desire for control an obsession, his adherence to ritual a mask for a pathetic deficiency of self-esteem.

What is beyond dispute is that, for whatever jumble of reasons, when the mowing is finished that April morning our man will be contented. He hurls the last boxful of cuttings on to the now gently steaming heap, and turns back to view with quiet complacency the effect of his stripes. He silences his machine and returns it to its place of rest, perhaps offering a tribute to its dependability as he wipes the cutters clean with an oily rag. He throws down his gloves, with their new stains of green, beats off the spattering of grass attached to his shins, stamps his

11

feet, becomes aware again of the extraordinary amount of noise birds make. He is ready to do battle in the supermarket, welcome a tiresome guest, play football with a clamorous son, attend to his beloved; to pick up again his spot in the society of human beings. He is strengthened by what he has done; and a good part of his comfort lies in the fact that – whether or not he is conscious of it at that moment – he must do the same next week, and the week after that, and every week until the earth again tires of making things grow.

PART ONE

In the Beginning

Care must be taken that the lawn is of such a size that about it in a square can be planted every sweet-smelling herb. Upon the lawn, too, against the heat of the sun, trees should be planted, so the lawn may have a delightful, cooling shade

ALBERTUS MAGNUS, Count of Bollstadt

I t is the rather tedious convention among gardening historians to begin with Genesis, which tells us that God created the first garden, eastward in Eden, and Adam the first gardener. The complacent assumption is that the Creator ordained gardening as humankind's pre-eminent recreation; that in the garden, of whatever kind, he gave a virtuous echo of that first perfect state; and that, by implication, the garden would for ever be a source of solace and spiritual improvement. Should we also presume that in Eden the essentials were provided: not merely the earth, the seed, water and warmth, and perhaps a useful implement or two; but also the aspiration to cultivate that rich soil in a manner pleasing to the eye and refreshing to the spirit?

The historians seize upon Genesis because it is somewhere to start, like a footpath sign. But scarcely have they taken the first steps along the path than it disappears into the dark, impenetrable tangle of Roman, Anglo-Saxon and early medieval Britain. They halt to scour the old chronicles, searching for a shard of light in the twilit thicket. But they are disappointed. There is enough evidence about life in first millennium Britain to show, for instance, that it was uncertain and often violent, that some held to the faith of Christ, that a minute handful could read and write, that amid the darkness the yearning to create beauty occasionally stirred and found expression. But of glimmers of interest in the garden as a diversion, the chronicles are almost bare. So they blunder on through the wildwood, until suddenly a shaft of sunlight does break through, and where it strikes the ground a sprig of green is visible.

They rush towards it, falling upon it with desperate relief; and at once begin constructing great edifices. A reference is found in the annals of Ely to the planting by Abbot Brithnod of gardens and orchards, which is taken as proof that a tradition of ecclesiastical horticulture was firmly in place before the end of the 10th century. In some dusty record of domestic purchases, a note is found to the effect that three-and-tenpence was spent on turf for the London garden of the Earl of Gloucester's curiously named brother, Bogo de Clare, from which is deduced a general enthusiasm among the 13th-century aristocracy for disporting themselves on cultivated grass. And from similarly nugatory smatterings are derived such absurdities as 'medieval men loved their flowers'. It would indeed be cheering to know that, in those brutish days, some knew their pinks and carnations, cherished mulberry and pear trees, even laid turves and lived long enough to see the grass grow. Perhaps there were knights who occasionally dismounted from their palfreys to pick nosegays for their ladies, and paused awhile, fumbling for a way to express their tender feelings in elegant prose. But we may be sure that feuding, fighting, intriguing, keeping their subordinates in order and promoting their good offices with their lord counted for a great deal more.

Go back almost two thousand years, to the heart of the Roman empire at its zenith, to Pliny's garden near Ostia, where you might have strolled between hedges of box and mulberry, listening to your host moralizing about the destruction of Pompeii; or to his Tuscan villa where the terrace sloped to a soft and liquid lawn, surrounded by paths and topiary, shaded by cypress and plane trees. Here, far removed from the noise of war, men's thoughts could turn to the pleasures of food and wine, and to beauty, the arts of poetry and sculpture, the taming of nature into a garden.

Go back a thousand years, to pre-Conquest Britain. Here, men laboured to exist, and generally did not exist very long. Sharing their wattle and mud hovels with their livestock and attendant multitudes of vermin, they rose at daybreak, toiled through the hours of daylight on the land, devoured their dismal sludge of beans and stewed vegetables, went to sleep; and did that most of the days of their adult lives. Nor was the existence of their feudal lords much more refined. Their homes may have been bigger, but they were just as draughty, dark and smelly. They ate much the same food and were eaten by the same fleas. True, they did not spend their days in manual drudgery. But the round of banditry, quarrelling, organizing and repelling raids, and the duties of providing and beseeching protection which alone offered any hope of stability in a turbulent world, can have left little enough daytime for anything much beyond sharpening battle axes and watching backs.

It is likely that a handful among the very richest among Britain's Roman rulers included ornamental gardens within their villas. Excavations at Fishbourne in Sussex have revealed that, in the centre of a resplendent first-century country house, was a courtyard laid out as a garden, with a walk flanked by ornamental arbours and shrubs, and possibly beds of violets, pansies, lilies and assorted herbs. At a humbler level, the Celtic monks most probably made gardens of a kind within their monasteries and beside their huts; and the greater religious institutions – such as Ely – may well have boasted more extensive cultivated grounds.

However, it was not until well after the coming of William and his Norman knights that the seedbed was laid on which the island's first civilizing influences would eventually germinate and flower. It took time to impose Norman order on a barbarian territory infected for centuries by chronic disorder, and much killing and brutality. But the slow, reluctant bowing of the Anglo-Saxon shoulder opened the way to blessings the land had never known, chief among which was an emerging confidence in freedom from invasion. The establishment of a structure of government, however harsh and oppressive it was, undoubtedly assisted the birth of an idea of nationhood, and with that, an aspiration to explore life's spiritual dimension.

We shouldn't make too much of this. For the labouring

classes of husbandmen and villeins, life continued to equate to toil. The demands of persuading the ground to provide enough to eat, and of rendering service to the lord, consumed existence. For those lords, life was certainly easier – and for their princes, easier still – but still uncertain and usually abbreviated. They made war, and played at it in their tournaments; adjudicated on the grievances of their retainers; organized the defence of their realms and plotted to subvert those of their rivals. Their chief sport was to chase and kill animals, a diversion which they pursued with terrific enthusiasm. That life might have a gentler, more contemplative side seems to have occurred to few of them.

But, the Norman order did provide for that side. Through the breach made by the warriors came the monks of Saint Benedict. They had built their great abbeys and accumulated their great estates in Normandy. Now they were invited to do the same in England. It was this engineered monastic revival which caused gardening's green shoots to show.

I used to know a man – later the editor of a well-known provincial newspaper – who told me in all seriousness that he had investigated a case in which an office worker from Slough had left his home one morning, walked a little way along the road and fallen through an unusual kind of hole into the 14th century. Whether he was lost for ever, or managed to find a way to reascend into our own age, I cannot now recall.

Were I to suffer a similar fate, and had I the choice among the variety of occupations open to men of the

Middle Ages, I think I could do worse than be *gardinarius* in a Benedictine monastery. Brother Thomas I would be, a person of middling status in the monastic hierarchy, unregarded beside the abbot, the prior, the bursar, the precentor and the other major obedientiaries. Doubtless the monks of the scriptorium, with their noses buried in bibles and psalters, would look down on me, with my rough, weathered hands and attendant odour of fish; although they would be grateful enough when executing their illuminations for the dyes derived from the berries and flowers grown under my direction.

Mine would be largely an outdoor life, and a most useful one. I would tend and jealously guard the monastery fishponds, watching over the carp, bream and pike, fattening them up with choice morsels until the feast day came and they were dispatched to the table to provide welcome relief from starch. I would, if there were a river, have an eel fishery; and trap them of a dark night in autumn when the migrating urge is on them, for no flesh of freshwater fish is richer or more tasty. I would have charge of the orchards, prune the apple and pear trees, tend to them at blossom time, gather in the fruit. I would know the way of bees and when to harvest their honey. I would know something of herbs and their ways, although their cultivation and medicinal use would probably be the responsibility of a specialist *infirmarius*. The sight of my vines would gladden my heart, and the thought of the wine they would provide would warm my spirit through the long hours of devotion and contemplation which the discipline demanded.

The physical well-being of the monastery would depend, in great measure, on me; and productivity and usefulness would surely be my guiding principles. But there would be more to it than that.

The theory of monastic life came from Saint Benedict: 'None follows the will of his own heart.' The practice meant a sufficiency of nourishment to sustain life, and little more; ample daily doses of organized communal devotion; a lot of hard work; and, during what was left from a monk's waking hours, peace, quiet, and a setting conducive to the meditative working of the mind. And they knew, those clever monks, how much more likely the human mind was to turn to the profitable pondering of God's mysteries if stimulated by God's work at its most evidently pleasing. Enfolded in the harmony of nature, soothed and delighted by the song of the birds and the rustle of the leaves, caressed by the scents of the flowers and herbs, open to all the associations of the paradise garden, the inner being could soar.

The famous Benedictine monastery blueprint found at St Gall in Switzerland, dating from the 9th century, confirms that the meditative heart of the monastery was the cloister garden, or garth. It was enclosed by one wall of the church, and by the communal buildings, the refectory and the monks' cells. The church was for observing the liturgy, while the open space of the garden was supposed to encourage the brothers' souls in private prayer and spiritual wrestling, to raise their vision from this world and its imperfections to the light made available in the Gospels of Christ.

Its ability to promote this influence was, in part, derived from its dominant colour. From the earliest times, green had symbolized rebirth, resurrection, fertility, happiness both temporal and spiritual. Brides in ancient Palestine wore green. The green of the Prophet Mohammed's cloak and of the banner beneath which he and his followers marched was the green of hope. But it is also the colour of tranquillity and refreshment. Long before modern science was able to establish that it is, indeed, the colour most restful to the eye because of the exactness with which it is focussed on the retina, the phenomenon had been accepted. In the 18th century Addison wrote: 'The rays that produce in us the idea of green fall upon the eye in such due proportion that they give the animal spirits their proper play.' A little later, the philosopher David Hartley defined the connection in his *Observations on Man*: 'The middle colour of the seven primary ones, and consequently most agreeable to the organ of sight, is also the general colour of the vegetable kingdom.'

The power of the colour was acknowledged by the chroniclers. In the records of the great monastery at Clairvaux, the sick man is seated upon a green lawn ('*sedet aegrotus cespite in viridi*'), and 'for the comfort of his pain all kinds of grass are fragrant in his nostrils . . . the lovely green of herb and tree nourishes his eyes'. The theme is taken up by Hugh of Fouilloy, who observes how 'the green turf . . . refreshes encloistered eyes, and their desire to study returns. It is truly the nature of the colour green that it nourishes the eyes and preserves their vision.'

On this basis – accepting that every visible trace of every medieval monastic garden was long ago expunged, and that no medievalist can know for sure what the physical reality of the monastic garden was – it is a reasonable assumption that it would have contained turf. Grass would have appeared of its own accord; and having done so, would have been approved as a generous, reliable supplier of the beneficence of green. These little patches, around which the cowled brothers shuffled murmuring from the Scriptures, or sat, eyes fixed upon the firmament, were the first lawns.

There is some evidence – a nod here and there among the old books and illustrations – to suggest that cultivated grass was a feature of the handful of pleasure gardens created outside the great ecclesiastical institutions. Henry II's garden at Clarendon in Wiltshire was said to boast 'a wealth of lawns'. Under Henry III, turf was laid at the Palace of Westminster, and a herbarium ordered by him at Windsor Castle may well have contained a lawn. A drawing of 1280, now in the British Museum, shows a game of bowls being played on what could be a rudimentarily levelled expanse of grass. A few years earlier, there is a record of a squire of Eleanor of Castile being paid threepence a night to water the turves at Conway Castle.

The date 1260 is honoured among historians who have sought to reassemble the long-buried elements of the medieval garden. In that year a Swabian nobleman turned Dominican friar, Albertus Magnus, Count of Bollstadt, produced the first gardening book, *De Vegetabilis*. And included in its wisdom – for which the name of Albertus Magnus should be blessed – are instructions for creating a lawn. The noble count counsels that the ground be cleared of weeds, flooded with boiling water and laid with turves which should be beaten down with 'broad mallets and trodden'; then the grass 'may spring

23

forth and closely cover the surface like a green cloth'. Those who have explored these recondite places more thoroughly than me – chiefly the late John Harvey, to whose work I am glad to pay tribute – believe that a similar species of pleasure garden, 'merry with green trees and herbs', was described a few years earlier by the encyclopaedist Bartholomew De Glanville, much of whose work was subsequently lost.

The digger in the past is mightily cheered by these nuggets. From them, it is clear that a primitive technique for nurturing grass did exist by the early 13th century. Someone had done it, others had copied him, adapting the methods, until a form of knowledge had coalesced to become sufficiently general for an educated man with a self-appointed mission to record the current condition of learning to include it. They are hardly more than names, Albertus and Bartholomew. But the fact that they wrote in Latin made their books as comprehensible in a monastery in East Anglia as in Dalmatia, Swabia or Rome. It is a pleasing fancy that, within the cloisters of Ely or Canterbury, some literate monk, emerging from a session of laborious copying in the scriptorium, might have encountered Brother Thomas the *gardinarius* (not much of a one for books, as you might gather from his earth-encrusted fingers and communion with carp), and passed on a couple of tips from the Swabian count on how to improve the scruffy condition of the grass in the cloister garth.

Although it is convenient and gratifying to refer to these assorted patches of green as lawns, it is anachronistic and a touch misleading. The Latin word used by Bartholomew is *pratum*, which is translated in English as 'mead', from the Old English *medwe*. The word 'lawn' is derived from the Old French *laund*, and was not known in the Middle Ages at all. According to the *Oxford English Dictionary*, it made its debut in Thomas Elyot's dictionary of 1548 – 'a place voyde of trees, as in a parke or forret'. It retained this meaning, of an open space between trees, in Johnson's dictionary of 1755, illustrated with lines from *Paradise Lost*:

> Betwixt them lawns, or level downs, and flocks
> Grazing the tender herb were interposed.

Actually, had the great lexicographer inquired a little more assiduously, he would have found that the word had already been particularized to a degree, being applied to an expanse of grass laid down by design in the vicinity of a house, with the purpose of enhancing its appearance. But, although there are examples of the word being used in that sense quite early in the 18th century – for instance in Miller's *The Garden Kalendar* of 1733 – the application was far from universal. Indeed, as late as 1833, in *The English Gardener*, Cobbett refers to such features as 'grass-plats'. Go back to Johnson, and you find these as 'grass-plots', defined as 'a small level covered with short grass', and illustrated with a line from Shakeapeare's *Tempest* – 'here on this grass-plot, in this very place, come and sport'.

If we then return to Bartholomew, we find him warbling about his meads 'y-hight with herb and grass and flowers of diverse kind. And therefore, for fairness and green springing that is within, it is y-said that meads laugheth.' This, then, is the medieval lawn, not notably kempt, the grass sparkling with daisies, violets, trefoil, speedwell. And having made the leap from the monastery, the concept of grass as something more than a source of food for sheep and cattle took hold in the developing English artistic consciousness. In Chaucer's *Legend of Good Women*, the good women disported themselves

> Upon the small, soft, sweet grass,
> that was with flowers sweet embroidered all
> of such sweetness and such odour all.

A few years later the unknown author of *The Floure and the Leafe* carolled in anaemic Chaucerian imitation of a herber

> that benched was, and with turves new
> freshly turved, whereof the grene gras
> so small, so thik, so short, so fresh of hew
> that most lyk to grene wol, wot I, it was.

This earthly paradise corresponds with that encountered by the travellers in Boccaccio's *Decameron* in the gardens of the Villa Palmieri near Florence – 'a meadow plot of green grass, powdered with a thousand flowers, set round with orange and cedar trees'.

The historian is properly grateful for these fragments. But, in the absence of any surviving medieval English garden, any detailed description of one, or any comprehensive work of instruction from which to make sound deductions, it is tempting to make much – perhaps too much – of the inherently unreliable evidence presented by poets and painters. This is not to suggest that Chaucer and lesser mortals were engaged in deliberate deceit.

But, in general, the purpose of art and literature was not to record the world as it was, but to present a brighter, more beautiful, divinely inspired vision; the world as it might be if God's creatures abandoned their vicious ways and lived according to his Word (the *Canterbury Tales* being, in part, the glorious exception).

It is difficult to believe that anyone who read the most popular European poem of the 14th century, Guillaume de Lorus's *Roman de la Rose*, can have related the interminable amorous gyrations of its courtly hero to anything happening in their own lives. This was the century of the Black Death, the Peasants' Revolt, the Hundred Years' War. Life was assaulted by the prospect of death by violence or putrefying disease, privation, starvation or social upheaval; and it was understandable that the artistic consciousness should have preferred to dwell in a clean, sweet-smelling, idealized kingdom of the imagination.

This is the setting for the *Roman de la Rose*, which Chaucer translated from the French. Here, freed from any obligation to engage with life, the courtier could devote himself to the intricacies of love-making, his delicate footsteps directed by the bloodless conventions of courtly love. He progresses, at the speed of a snail, towards his fulfilment, enacted in the centre of a garden in the form of a perfect square, with a fountain at the intersection of its diagonals. The sky is blue, the air warm, the cheeks of the participants untouched by mark of pox, their clothes neat and clean, the birds a-twitter, the trees in blossom, the grass lush and spangled with violets and periwinkles and flowers red and yellow – 'such plenty there grew never in mead', Chaucer writes. In the 15th-century illustrations of the poem in the British Museum, we see the courtly company loose in this Eden, prancing around to the strains of harp, oboe and fife-and-drums, beneath their feet a soft carpet of vegetation, their milk-white faces shaded by luxuriant trees.

It is a world of complete make-believe, purged of ugliness. We meet it in Stefan Lockner's *Madonna in the Rose Arbour*, in which the grass is studded with daisies, violets, red clover and strawberries; in the Hennesy *Book of Hours*, where the saints Cosmos and Damian are seated on a turf bench in the middle of a lawn bright with daisies and camomile; in a fresco of Pinturicchio showing Susannah and the Elders against a background of turf and flowers; in the tapestry known as the *Lady with the Unicorn*, where the lady receives a jewelled necklace from her maid, standing in a flowery mead.

I encountered it on my honeymoon, in the chapel built in Granada to contain the remains of the Catholic monarchs, Ferdinand and Isabella. It was a Flemish painting of the early 15th century, displaying a fine palace, a garden in which squares of grass are divided by gravel paths, a low wall with peacocks on it, a couple reading under a tree, a knot with spindly trees, a lake with a swan and sloping lawns leading down to it, the grass shorn rather than shaggy.

So medieval man, or our time parachutist, would have found lawns in the imaginary world of poetry, painting and tapestry; and might have encountered a version of the real thing within the great ecclesiastical institutions, and adorning royal pleasure grounds. But to believe a stroll around the countryside would have brought him,

28

sooner or later, to a well-ordered garden containing cultivated grass is probably fanciful. Miles Hadfield, in his
History of British Gardening, asserts that gardening as an
aesthetic pursuit did not exist in England before the end
of the 15th century. He dismisses attempts to cite the
walled and trellised gardens of the *Roman de la Rose* illustrations, arguing that the presence of such exotics as
dates, liquorice and zedoary reflects a purely Continental
tradition. Energetic medievalists necessarily disagree,
maintaining that, with the development of international
commerce, Continental influences must have achieved
a degree of penetration; and that, anyway, the division
between serviceable and aesthetic is false.

To put this argument simplistically, medieval man
would have grown his apples and pears to eat or sell
them, his leeks and garlic to make soup, his thyme and
hyssop and sage to flavour his food and treat his ailments,
his vines to make wine. And in the planting and the
growing and the harvesting, he would have taken a spiritual pleasure; smiled at the blossom, breathed in the
fragrance, felt the fatness of grapes in his hand; and,
consciously or unconsciously, he would have found that
there was a correlation between the arrangement of his
garden and the degree of his pleasure.

It is a truism to observe that the period between the
Norman Conquest and the victory of Henry VII on Bos-
worth Field gave birth to the nation, and hazardous to
offer generalizations about national psychology. On the
other hand, an attempt has to be made to explain how
the aspiration to create order and beauty achieved physical expression. Norman rule freed England from what
had been the constant threat of invasion. But it took

time for the effects of this liberation to percolate the collective consciousness. The ruling class continued to organize their demesnes on the first principle that they must be resistant to attack. Any garden ordered by the lord for his gratification had, therefore, to be contained within fortified walls. But as time went on, and notions of permanence and stability of a sorts took hold, so was born a new confidence; and, for the first time, the lord considered the possibility of enclosing his lordly dwelling within its grounds, rather than the other way round. Freed at last from the psychic claustrophobia imposed by fear of chaos, the human spirit might take wing and, recalling Eden, create a garden.

With confidence came a mighty economic growth, which the depredations of the wars with France, the astounding population cull of the Black Death, and assorted social upheavals, merely slowed, never halted. Although the great mass of the population remained mired in the unending struggle for survival, significant numbers, inspired by the possibility of self-advancement, rose like bubbles in a dark pond to take their places among the élite. Trade with Continental Europe, particularly in wool and woven cloth, soared. Huge fortunes were made, and required managing and spending. Great men had leisure, as they always had. But now they had more idea what to do with it, though hunting, hawking and playing war games remained their chief outlets.

With wealth came a loosening of the ropes which bound people to their protectors and the places where they were born. No longer did they feel so inclined to share their living quarters with their livestock and toil on soil which was not theirs, for the benefit of remote, grasping landlords. Nor were they edified by the spectacle of privileged prelates and the vast army of lesser clergy feasting on the proceeds of their tithes. As the abbots and bishops and friars exchanged devotion to their vows for ever softer living, so did the reputation of their Church decline. In the great religious houses, even the humble *gardinarius* would have his servant, and perhaps a dovecote to cluck over, and a dog to take scraps. They were no longer sanctuaries from barbarism, but places of frequently ostentatious luxury, the maintenance of which required endless cadging and knavish tricks.

The new-found social fluidity engendered a spiritual flowering. No longer apprehensive about what the next day might bring, nor owing obeisance to a feudal lord or vainglorious bishop, educated Tudor man looked around him. Settled in his fine house, his lands secure, with cash to spare, he wanted more from life than merely its continuation. Staring from his gabled windows out over his acres, his curiosity stirred. It was time for the first gardening book in English.

Pleasures of the Green

These even and uniform carpets of green velvet, seen through their countryside, which other nations have not been able to obtain for themselves, make an admirable sight. People tried vainly to imitate them in France . . . the lawns that grow in France are not fine

ANTOINE JOSEPH DEZALLIER D'ARGENVILLE

Actually, that first 'pleasant treatise' of Thomas Hill, published in the first year of Elizabeth's rule, 1558, does not – except for the chronicler searching for serviceable milestones – mark the beginning of anything; and since he has nothing to say about grass beyond the observation that turfed walks provide comfort and delight for the wearied mind, he need not detain us long. The interest of the little book lies not so much in the ragbag of other people's experience and prejudice drawn together by its energetic compiler, but – as Hadfield points out – as an indicator of a public appetite. Gardening had begun to take root in Tudor England. People wanted to know from Thomas Hill 'how to dress, sow and set a garden; and what remedies may be had and used against such beasts, worms and flies and such like that annoy gardens'. And they existed in sufficient numbers to make it worth Hill's time to sift through the assorted tedious teachings of 'Palladius, Columella, Varro, Pyophanes, learned Cato and many more', to pick out the nuggets which might be usefully applied in his damp, temperate land, and – in his own word – 'English' them.

The first English writer to whom the lawnsman owes a bow of respect is Gervase Markham, whose *The English Husbandman* of 1613 (later refined and expanded into *Cheap and Good Husbandry*) made available a coherent programme of action to make best use of English earth. There is charm and sense in Markham's counsel:

> The mixture of colours is the only delight of the eye above all others . . . as in the composition of a delicate woman, the grace of her cheeks is the mixture of red and white, the wonder of the eye black and white, and the beauty of her hand blue and white, any of which is not said to be beautiful if it consist of single or simple colours; and so in these walks and alleys the all green, nor the all yellow, cannot be said to be the most beautiful, but the green and the yellow (that is the untrod grass and the well-knit gravel) being equally mixed, give the eye lustre and delight beyond all comparison.

The point is well made, in its roundabout fashion.

Markham's recipe for producing that green to delight the eye is none the less valid for its close resemblance to that advocated by that sound old Swabian, Albertus Magnus. Cleanse the ground of stones and weeds, destroy the roots – in how many manuals of lawn care have those arduous principles been recycled? Gervase Markham (or Albertus) was there first. Boiling water should be poured all over, he says; then the floor beaten 'and trodden mightily'. Place 'turfs of earth full of green grass, the bare earth turned upwards', then 'dance upon with the feet' until the grass 'may begin to peep up and put forth small hairs . . . until finally it is made the sporting green plot for ladies and gentlemen to recreate their spirits in'. Hats off and raised spades to Gervase Markham, for even now one could do worse! And how pleasant is the picture of those Jacobean enthusiasts capering upon their upturned turves, and reaping their reward a year or two later, as they stroll forth with their ladies across the soft grass, stopping to play chess or 'recreate their spirits' with some verses of Spenser.

How extensively Markham's advice was observed, we cannot tell. What we do know is that, by his time, it had become common for aristocrats and plutocrats to commission bowling greens in their grounds, as well as turfed and gravelled walks. By the early 17th century the game of bowls was already secure in the affections of all levels of society. Indeed, Richard II had banned it on the grounds that it was distracting the people from archery, and a Frenchman was never going to be downed by a flying bowl. The prohibition was renewed by Henry IV and Edward IV, and re-imposed by Henry VIII, who declared: 'The game of bowls is an evil because the alleys are in operation in conjunction with saloons or dissolute places . . . a vicious form of gambling'. Innkeepers were threatened with a fine of two pounds for permitting the game to be played. But – perhaps because Henry himself was known to be a keen and accomplished player – little attention seems to have been paid, and bowls continued to flourish.

In medieval times, it was generally played on flattened

cinders or clay. But by 1600, grass had become the pre-ferred surface for the nobility and gentry (although it is thought likely that Drake played his immortal game on an expanse of camomile). An elementary science of grass culture must have evolved, too; the greens must have been as flat as they could make them, and the grass as short and thick and even as they could get it. By 1670 the rules of bowls had been formalized, and a few years later Randle Holme wrote in the *Academy of Armory* that 'bowling greens are open wide spaces made smooth and even ... orders agreed by gentlemen bowlers that noe high heeles enter for spoiling their green, they forfeit sixpence'.

We can only speculate whether similar standards of care were translated to the ornamental grass plot; whether the Elizabethans and Jacobeans cared if it were flat or bumpy, whether they liked flowers and herbs inter-mingled, how often they cut and rolled, and how. In the absence of any surviving garden of the period, we again have to rely upon the ancient texts and illustrations, in which – regrettably – the attention paid to grass and its cultivation is at best fleeting, and at worst non-existent. If we wish, we can learn a good deal about their affection for the intricacies of the knot and the maze, and the eagerness with which they seized upon the fruits of explo-ration and commerce – not just the potato, but cedars, laburnums, tulips, yuccas, Jerusalem artichokes, oranges, lemons, cherries and a host of new flowers and shrubs. England was more prosperous than it had ever been, and more stable – until the Civil War – than any country in Europe had ever been. Men were inspired by the questing spirit, and gardening's experimental, organic character made it a natural outlet. Sadly but understandably, that spirit was rarely exercised by the matter of grass. There was, however, one notable exception.

The authentic voice of late Elizabethan and early Jacobean England is that of Francis Bacon, Viscount St Albans, one of the numerous distinctions of whose life was that it was ended by a chill caught while he was stuffing a dead fowl with snow to observe the effect of cold on the preservation of flesh. It is characteristic of the elasticity of Bacon's mind that, in the midst of half a lifetime's unscrupulous and serpentine manoeuvrings at court – whose sole guiding principle was the promotion of his own interests – he should have published his *Essays*, or *Counsell Civill and Morall*, which amounted to a manual of spiritual and cultural self-improvement. The range of these homilies, the richness of the learning they display, and the elegance of their prose, are amazing. But equally remarkable is the tone, its authority and confidence. Whether in routing the atheists, measuring the usefulness of novelties, or analysing the fruits of friendship, this supreme know-all is immune to the very notion of uncertainty.

Bacon's intellectual arrogance is on magnificent display in his famous essay 'Of Gardens'. In considering the garden, he does not stoop to concern himself with anything so mundane as the growing of things. His mind is on the moral dimension. The garden is, he asserts, 'the purest of human pleasures . . . the greatest refreshment to the spirit of man'. 'When ages grow to civility and elegance, men come to build stately sooner than to garden finely as if gardening were the greater perfection.' The regulations are set out with impregnable assurance. Bacon scorns knots with 'diverse coloured earths' as toys. Images cut in juniper or 'other garden stuff' are for children. Aviaries are impermissible. Pools 'marr all and make the garden unwholesome and full of frogs and flies'. The main garden must be square, surrounded by a 'stately arched hedge', with turrets above the arches to contain bird-cages. At each end of the side gardens there should be a mound, breast high; and at the centre of the whole thing, another, thirty feet high, with three ascents, each broad enough for four to walk abreast; and within the hedged alleys should be gravelled walks (not grass, which would be 'going wet').

Bacon's ideal Eden in St Albans – it's difficult to imagine him or anyone else actually creating and maintaining such an exorbitance – covered thirty acres. There were three essential elements: at the far end, a natural wilderness devoid of trees but rampant with thickets of sweet briar and honeysuckle; in the middle, the main garden; at the entrance, the green. Here is our first true English lawn:

> The green hath two pleasures, the one, because nothing is more pleasant to the eye than green grass kept finely shorn; the other, because it will give you a fair alley in the midst, by which you may go in front upon a stately hedge which is to enclose the garden.

That is all. There is no hint as to how the precept is to be realized. The fount of wisdom does not dirty his hands with practical tips. For those we must consult our plodding friend, Gervase Markham. And in any case, it seems most improbable that this four acres of perfect turf ever existed outside Bacon's imagination. That is not the point. The significance of Bacon's essay on gardens lies, not in any practical application, but in the fact that he wrote it. It proves that, by the turn of the 16th century, the cultured Englishman's apprehension of how to express himself included the concept of the decorative garden, and that an expanse of cultivated grass was fundamental to that concept. By and large, it has remained so ever since. And as Englishmen took ever greater pride in their Englishness, developing as a national pastime the habit of comparing themselves favourably to foreigners, so did they learn to see grass, not merely as a contributor to the beauty and harmony of the pleasure garden but, as of itself, another symbol and symptom of English superiority.

Sir Henry Wooton, diplomat, Provost of Eton, angler, scholar, poet, spent most of his adult life serving his country's interests in the capitals of Europe. He studied our neighbours closely, learned their languages, became familiar with their habits, and concluded, with that quiet, unassailable certitude which over the centuries so impressed and irritated those who encountered it: 'In our own country there is a delicate and diligent curiosity surely without parallel among foreign nations.' Another eminent and complacent polymath, Sir William Temple, identified evidence of that divinely bestowed pre-eminence:

> Besides the temper of our climate, there are two things particular to us that contribute much to the beauty and elegance of our gardens, which are the gravel of our walks and the fineness and almost per-

petual greenness of our turf . . . which cannot be found in France or Holland as we have it, the soil not admitting that fineness of blade in Holland, nor the sun that greenness in France . . .

Pepys subscribed wholeheartedly to what had clearly become a general assumption: 'We have the best gravel walks in the world, France having none nor Italy; and the green of our bowling alleys is better than any they have.'

Is it any wonder that, meeting such impregnable smugness, visitors from continental Europe should have been moved to occasional outbursts against English arrogance? The paradox – one might say the hypocrisy – of this island pride is that it should have been accompanied by an extremely enlightened openness to Continental influence; an eagerness to purloin, adapt and improve upon the discoveries of others, and then pass them off as Anglo-Saxon inspirations. The extent to which post-Restoration garden design in England was shaped by, even copied from, the example realized with such overpowering magnificence in France is a matter hotly and inconclusively debated by the historians. The prosecution case is persuasive, resting as it does on the certain facts that, as a cousin of Louis XIV and a frequent visitor to his court during the years of exile, Charles II must have observed the unfolding in the Tuileries of André Le Nôtre's grandiose geometric vision of a royal garden; that, on becoming king, Charles asked his cousin if he might borrow Le Nôtre, then engaged at Fontainebleau; that, although Le Nôtre probably never came, his precepts were put into practice at St James's Park by André Mollet, whose father had worked with Le Nôtre.

The French tradition was founded on a delight in, and dependence on, geometric patterns. The lines are drawn by channels of water, by hedges and avenues of trees, by paths – all of undeviating straightness. Within the angles of intersection are arranged in symmetrical harmony all manner of attractions: fountains, flower beds, arbours, pools, grass plots and so on. All are where they are according to a grand design. For the first time, the garden becomes an overt statement of Man's ambition and ability to control the world around him and make it reflect his image. In the case of the gardens of the Sun King, it may well be that what seems to us now their chilly and regimented splendour was the projection of the proprietor rather than their designer. But since neither Louis nor Le Nôtre – nor indeed, I'm sorry to say, King Charles – evinced any interest in the cultivation of grass, we need not dwell on their ambitions.

Others were more enlightened, and inclined to resist the French model. John Worlidge, in his *Art of Gardening* (1677) bemoaned the influence of the 'new, useless and unpleasant mode', denounced the banishment of 'garden flowers, the miracles of nature', contending that the French system of gravel walks and grass plots was fit for kings and princes only. He celebrated the delight taken in their gardens by Englishmen of all classes, the noble in his country seat, the shopkeeper with his 'boxes, pots and other receptacles, plants etc.', the cottage dweller with his 'proportionable garden'.

Worlidge was an early pragmatist. Far removed from court circles, free from any need to fawn and flatter, he knew perfectly well that the vast spread of Versailles with its armies of gardeners was no sort of an example for an

Englishman. For him gardening's proper companion was common sense rather than high ambition. His approach – and that of his equally sensible contemporary, John Rea – was severely practical. Rea's *Flora* of 1665 honoured on an epic scale the glories of flower, plant and fruit (the fashionable delight in patterns of grass and gravel, to the exclusion of all else, he damned as 'an immoral nothing').

Buried within its mass of instruction is some scanty advice about laying turf with a turfing iron, and disciplining it with a 'heavy, broad Beater'. Rea's tips echo those in the other influential guide of the time, John Evelyn's *Kalendarium Hortense*. Evelyn is remembered these days, if at all, for his voluminous diary which was discovered in an old clothes basket at his home more than a hundred years after his death. In his time he was famed as the first great advocate of tree planting, and a dispenser of generally sound, if exceedingly wordy, gardening lore. He tells the lawnsman that in October 'it will now be good to beat, roll and mow . . . for the ground is supple and it will even all inequalities'.

It is improbable that a rich landowner such as Evelyn, or literate gentlemen such as Rea and Worlidge, would have done anything more strenuous in their gardens than giving the orders; so perhaps we should excuse their reticence on technical matters, annoying though it is. Beating was done with a mallet, rolling with a roller not materially different from our own. Mowing deserves a closer look.

The word is Old English, the science as ancient as the most ancient Egyptians, who used a sickle adapted from an animal's jawbone to harvest their corn. The Romans used a one-handed implement and stooped to cut. But the Englishman of the Middle Ages preferred to stand up straight, wielding a scythe almost as long as himself. It had two handles attached to its slightly curved willow snead, and a long blade of soft metal at right angles, which was sharpened with a block of sandstone.

Efficient scything demanded – beyond the stamina to keeping swinging through the long days of harvest-time – precision, dexterity and a harmony between man, his tool and his task. Until the machine age consigned him to redundancy, the scytheman was highly valued, and there was a romantic appeal to him and his labour. His oneness with landscape excited writers seeking to distil its essence; most notably Tolstoy, who devoted a memorable passage in *Anna Karenina* to Levin's spiritual flight into the boundless golden cornfields, where – scythe in hand – he mixed his sweat with that of the serfs as he tasted again the old bond with Mother Earth.

On a more modest scale, the poet Andrew Marvell explored the metaphorical possibilities:

> I am the mower, Damon, known
> Through all the meadows I have mown.

Despite presumably well-paid work and a healthy outdoor way of life, Damon is not happy. Love, of course, has made him so:

> Sharp like his scythe his sorrow was
> And wither'd like his Hopes the Grass.

Marvell makes play with his conceit:

> . . . she
> What I do to the grass, does to my Thoughts and Me.

The poem reaches an absurd climax, as:

> The edged Stele by careless chance
> Did into his Ankle glance.

The physical hurt Damon repairs, with 'Shepherd's-purse and Clowns-all-heal'. But there is a deeper cut, for which no cure this side of the grave can heal:

> Til death has done that this must do,
> For Death, thou art a Mower too.

Marvell's lines –

> While thus he threw his Elbow round,
> Depopulating all the ground,
> And, with his whistling scythe does cut
> Each stroke between the Earth and Root

– are the closest to a description of 17th-century scything that I have been able to discover; and, of course, refer to corn and meadow grass rather than anyone's grass plot. Clues about the tending of these are provided in a collection of drawings of garden tools executed by Evelyn to illustrate what was to have been his life's crowning work, his *Elysium Britannicum*, a survey of his native land and its achievements envisaged on such a massive scale that his energies were exhausted before it had advanced much beyond the planning stage. These include a group of implements for the lawn: a turf-lifter, a turf-edger and a scythe.

We must assume that this was how it was done. That it was done, that by the end of the 17th century the cultivation of fine grass in the form of bowling green or ornamental lawn had become general practice in the gardens of the great and the rich, is given some circumstantial weight by the accounts of that endlessly curious and untiring traveller, Celia Fiennes. In Mrs Stevens's 'neat gardens' at Epsom, she found six grass walks guarded by dwarf fruit trees; at Durdans in Surrey 'three long grass walks which are also very broad'; at Woburn a large bowling green with eight arbours, and a seat in a high tree where she sat and ate 'a great quantity of the Red Carolina gooseberry'. Visiting New College, Oxford, in 1694, Miss Fiennes much admired a great mound 'ascended by degrees in a round of green paths', and noted a bowling green.

Thirty years later the celebrated Oxford antiquarian Thomas Hearne lamented the rage for lawns. He noted sourly in his journal the destruction of the 'fine, pleasant garden' at Brasenose 'purely to turn it into a grass plot and erect some silly statue there'. As early as the 1670s, Christchurch, richest and grandest of the Oxford colleges, had enclosed a smooth, green lawn intersected by gravel paths, and reached by a noble flight of baroque steps. The fellows of Pembroke had their bowling green, while at Trinity College, Cambridge, Newton's feet trod soft turf as his mind wrestled with the mysteries of gravitational pull and refrangibility.

It would be absurd to pretend that the gardeners of the later Stuart period were at all excited by the subject of grass culture – or, I suppose, to suggest that the real gardeners of any period have been. Thus, despite Sir William Temple's already quoted tribute to English turf, it does not figure in his long, lyrical description of the garden at Moor Park where he spent his honeymoon in 1655: the 'perfectest figure of a garden I ever saw', with its gravelled terrace running along the house, its three flights of steps down to a rectangular parterre

44

quartered by gravel walks and bounded by cloisters, its grotto, fountains, statues, summer house, abundance of fruit trees and marked absence of flowers. The gardens of the Russells at Woburn at least boasted that bowling green. But it was the flower and vegetable gardens, and particularly the orchards (in 1674 fifteen different species of plum and twelve of pear were planted) which received the attention of the head gardener, John Field.

Passion was excited by the great advances in the science of botany and the ever-increasing availability of new plants. That ardour for the new triggered by pioneers such as the Tradescants, father and son, had enormously expanded the horticultural horizon. But on the whole, the grandees who commissioned the great gardens were not that exercised by subtle distinctions between varieties of gillyflower or nasturtium (although tulips, notoriously, were another matter). They were more inclined to involve themselves in novelties such as statuary and hydraulic engineering, and, in particular, topiary. The new king and queen, William and Mary, had brought with them from Holland their fondness for evergreen hedges and bushes, which clamoured for some artist with a pair of shears to work them into a resemblance of a camel or a griffin or some other diverting shape.

The desire common to the great men, of course, was that their trappings – including their gardens – should reflect and display their greatness. As is the way with the species, whatever image of greatness one great man presented to the world, another would seek to surpass it. Few strove harder, at greater expense and with more magnificent if ridiculous results, than James Brydges, successively Lord Chandos, Earl of Carnarvon, Viscount Wilton and Duke of Chandos, whose name is perpetuated in the series of anthems written in his honour by Handel.

The man who thought nothing of commissioning the greatest composer of the age to sing his praises had a home to match his estimation of his own importance, and gardens in proportion. The main parterre at Canons in Middlesex was studded with life-size statues, most prominent among them a gladiator who stood beside a canal fed with water piped from springs at Stanmore two miles away. The divisions of the parterre, most unusually, were of decorative ironwork. Vegetables were grown under beehives of glass. At the end of each of the eight intersecting alleys was a lodging for a retired army sergeant who, together, formed a guard for the place. There were flamingos, ostriches and blue macaws, and eagles which drank from stone basins. Tortoises from Majorca crept through the undergrowth, in little danger of straying outside the boundaries of an estate each of whose main avenues of trees was more than half a mile long. And there was turf at Canons, grown from seed imported, for reasons which remain obscure, from Aleppo. It must have thrived and been extensive, for when Chandos's fortunes were at their zenith, it was scythed three times a week and weeded daily.

Miles Hadfield suggests a close correspondence between the layout of the gardens at Canons and an influential book entitled *The Theory and Practice of Gardening,* first published in 1713 under the name John James, for many years Clerk to the Works at Greenwich. This was, in fact, a fairly close translation of a work by a Parisian, Antoine Joseph Dezallier D'Argenville, who had studied with a pupil of the great Le Nôtre, and was, therefore, a text-book for an essentially French school of design.

To be honest, there is little pleasure to be had from studying *The Theory and Practice* today. It is as short on charm and humour as Hillard and Botting's *First Latin Primer*. But one can understand why John James's cluster of aristocratic subscribers were so taken with it. It presents, not reflections or suggestions or philosophical aspirations, but prescriptions, precisely plotted and illustrated with encyclopaedic thoroughness. There are pages and pages of elaborate designs to choose from, which offer – or appear to – a guarantee of success. At the same time, the book does have, in its pedagogic fashion, dirty fingers. The nobleman, desirous of stamping the reflection of his nobility on his domain, might select a suitable rectangular plan. His head gardener, assuming he could read, could then learn how to put it all into practice. No one before had made available such a reliable, all-encompassing code of gardening conduct.

Anyone interested in the evolution of the lawn and grass culture has particular reason to be grateful to Mr James of Greenwich, for he tackles the subject with great thoroughness – or, perhaps, one should say that D'Argenville does. But, curiously enough, while the main design fundamentals expounded in *The Theory and Practice* are undoubtedly French in origin and inspiration, the section dealing with grass is not. D'Argenville graciously concedes the case:

47

> You cannot do better than follow the method used
> in England, where their grass plots are of so exquisite
> a beauty that in France we can scarcely hope to come
> up with it.

The essence of the overall doctrine is what James calls 'contrariety' – the 'placing and distributing the several parts of the garden always to oppose them one to the other'. It would be tedious to delve into the detail of its application. Suffice to say that the importance of turf is properly recognized. 'A bowling green', James reflects, 'is one of the most agreeable compartments of a garden and when 'tis rightly placed, nothing is more pleasant to the eye.' It demands, he adds, 'a beautiful carpet of turf very smooth and of a lovely green'. He proceeds to a succession of alternative plans, each presented with immense care. In one, the square of the green is edged in box and pierced with a star of paths, with a rounded hollow at the centre. Another is oval, 'cut in Carts to make a diversity'. There is a Great Bowling Green, 'adorned with a Buffet of Water made against the slope'; and an even greater one with compartments 'cut and tied together by Knots and Cartoozes of Embroidery, very delicate'.

In the Jamesian garden, the principal feature is the parterre (French, derived from the Latin *partire*, to divide), which was regularly shaped, usually edged in box, and intricately designed in patterns of gravel, sand, box, flowers, shrubs, trees or grass. The grass parterre was known as the 'parterre à l'Angloise', and should, according to the master, 'consist only of large grass plots all of a piece, or cut but little'.

These days the exemplars on which the Frenchman

and his English disciple lavished such care are no more than historical curiosities; symptoms of a preoccupation with orderliness and control which seems almost obsessive. But John James's instructions on how to get things to grow contained many of the eternal truths. All subsequent manuals on creating a lawn – up to and including those of our own Doctor Hessayon – elaborate on the principles laid down almost three hundred years ago. The ground should be dry, broken up, the stones raked and removed. A 'good mold' should be thrown on. Flat ground should be seeded, slopes turfed. The seed should be sown very thickly, then raked in. 'Chuse a mild day rather inclined to wet,' says *The Theory and Practice*, 'that the rain, forcing down the earth and sinking the seed, may cause it to shoot up the sooner. Do it in autumn rather than spring which can require continual waterings which is a very great slavery and expense.'

These are, quite simply, the immutable fundamentals of making a lawn. Nor is the master any less sound on the pitfalls. 'All the difficulty of making a fine green plot by sowing has in getting good seed.' He delivers a stern warning: 'You should not do, as many, that will gather their seed from some hayloft and sow it without distinction . . . the seed shooting too high, making large stalks, the lower part remains naked and bare, and mow it as often as you will it will never make handsome grass.' James is vague on where you should obtain your seed; understandably, since a century and a half later gardening writers were still bemoaning the difficulty in finding decent seed. Turf, he says, should be taken from road sides or from the edges of pastures and meadows where cows and sheep feed.

Regrettably, the Jamesian advice on maintaining grass is somewhat skimpy. Beat it when it gets too high, roll it with 'great cylinders or rolls of wood or stone', and mow it 'at least once a month'. These are the rules, and there is nothing wrong with them. But suspicions stir when the master proclaims: 'It ought to be so close and even that no one blade should exceed another.' Here, he succumbs to the proclivity of experts through the ages: for setting a completely unachievable target as if it were the easiest thing in the world, and intimating that it is merely our inadequacy or inattention which prevents us from emulating them. I would have enjoyed witnessing John James's technique with the scythe, checking the condition of his sward, and perhaps pointing out to him that the occasional blade was a few millimetres at variance with its neighbour.

The last edition of John James's book was published in 1743. By then fashion had moved on at a gallop. The design of gardens had become absorbed into a new cultural landscape and had become an issue for dispute. A generation of controversialists had come of age, thriving on the mockery and demolition of the traditions and tastes it had inherited. By 1743 the Duke of Chandos's monumental extravagance at Canons had mouldered into something approaching disrepair, His Grace's exchequer having been ruinously depleted by unsuccessful speculation (he died a year later, to be succeeded by his son Henry, who is reputed to have purchased one of his wives from an ostler as he was passing through Newbury). In a historical context, the more ludicrous aspects of the Duke's *folie de grandeur*, and the reaction to them, can be seen as marking a turning point.

But the fact that John James and his publishers considered it worthwhile to issue a new edition of *The Theory and Practice* thirty years after the first illuminates a rather inconvenient aspect of gardening in Britain. For obvious reasons, historians seek to identify, within whatever great or trivial subject they are tackling, climacterics which can justify those satisfying words: 'It was the end of an era.' But in concentrating on the innovations of the innovators, the proclamations and passings of the prophets, it is easy to overlook the extreme slowness with which many changes in taste take hold. This characteristic is particularly pronounced in gardening, because of the gap between concept and realization, dictated by the speed at which plants mature.

Thus, long after the start of what the history books tell us was a new age in English gardening, ordinary Englishmen were still turning to John James to find out what they should be doing with their patch of land. They are forgotten, and in almost all cases the evidence of what they did with their gardens has been expunged. But they – the great majority among the tiny minority of the population who made gardens – continued to pay more attention to the precepts laid down in *The Theory and Practice* than to anything being trumpeted forth by the new pioneers.

However, it seems improbable that John James's blueprints were duplicated across the land. Gardeners then would have done what gardeners of all ages do. They would have taken what was useful to them, what interested them and was applicable to their circumstances, financial as well as geographical; and ignored the rest. They would have learned through their own trial and error what in his theory and practice suited them. And if, having invested their time and money and love, they had discovered that the garden they had made had gone out of fashion, would they have hastened to dig it all up and start again?

Shaven Lawns and
Vapid Greens

*Grass is hard and lumpy and damp and full of dreadful
black insects*

OSCAR WILDE

During the 18th century, in reaction to principles of garden design imported from France, and under a Royal Family borrowed from Germany, a native, truly English style of marrying a house with its surroundings was born and came of age. Its apostles and disciples left an imprint on the land which endures in a recognizable form to the present day. They also stamped an impression on the national consciousness, a notion of Englishness, which took a powerful hold. I cannot claim that cultivated grass was a dominant motif; these men's minds were set on higher things. But grass, its texture, its colour, and its convenience, did become an indispensable element of the great Georgian garden. They did not think a great deal of it. But they found that that they could not do without it.

The new movement was, of course, invented by and largely confined to a minute sliver atop society's heap. The great illiterate mass of the population continued to do what they had always done with whatever land they had: to exploit it for dietary and medicinal purposes, and take delight in commonly available flowers and other plants. What we think of as the Georgian Garden was funded by a handful of enlightened aristocrats, executed by a few artists of taste and education who had a living to earn, and publicized by a crew of poets and prose writers accidentally infected by the passion.

The watchword of these arbiters of taste was 'Nature'. They looked at the rigid lines, the geometric patterns, the dry symmetries so beloved of the preceding generation, and recoiled. They studied the hedges and trees shaped by sharp shears into quadrilateral figures or fabulous animals, and laughed. In the first famous broadside, delivered in the pages of the *Spectator* in 1712, Addison wrote: 'Our British gardeners, instead of humouring Nature, love to deviate from it as much as possible. Our trees rise in cones, globes and pyramids. We see the marks of the scissors upon every plant and bush.'

What they meant by Nature had very little to do with the dark, tangled forests and dreary wastes of bog and rock which had been the natural condition of Britain until man got to work on it. They feared the savagery of the wilderness as much as their distant and immediate ancestors had. Their endeavour, in Pope's famous words, was to

Consult the genius of the place in all.

The genius of that resonant sentiment is that it was capable of almost any interpretation. It licensed Lord Burlington to annihilate topiary, parterres, knots and gravel paths, and put in their place temples and obelisks

54

copied from the monuments in the gardens of the Villa Borghese and Villa Aldobrandini which he had seen on his Grand Tour. It gave the nod of approval to the Temple of the Four Winds which Vanbrugh deposited on a windswept elevation at Castle Howard in Yorkshire; to the Merlin's Cave which Kent hid in the grounds of Richmond Palace; to Charles Bridgeman's amphitheatre at Claremont; to almost anything which aped the classical and proceeded in other than straight lines.

Pope expressed his philosophy more completely in Windsor Forest:

> Here hills and vales, the woodland and the plain,
> Here earth and water seem to strive again,
> Not chaos-like together crush'd and bruis'd,
> But, as the world, harmoniously confused.

The antithesis between 'not chaos-like . . . but harmoniously confused' is clever. It clears the way for Man to pursue the dictates of his imagination: the sole source – in the absence of direct divine involvement – of the harmony which can quieten pandemonium.

The mind of the little poet was as devious as the celebrated garden he created for himself beside the Thames at Twickenham, where he realized his own vision of beauty. Here, Pope would stroll from his grotto past his temple of shells along a grove of lime trees, pause awhile on the soft turf of his bowling green, inspect the obelisk put up in memory of his mother, inhale the scents of his orangery and finally seat himself in his garden house, where, enclosed by harmonious confusion, he would consider which of the innumerable targets of his vindictive disdain he would ridicule that fine day.

Pope seems to have been a genuinely dedicated and expert gardener. Bridgeman worked with him at Twickenham. Burlington was his friend. William Kent, the instrument of Burlington's Palladian ambitions, may have lent a hand. When Pope proclaimed a view of what men of taste should be doing with their money, men of taste listened. When he put the boot into those he decreed were without taste, his victims and their schemes were derided. This he did to Chandos and his folly at Canons:

> His gardens next your admiration call,
> On any side you look, behold the wall!
> No pleasing intricacies intervene,
> No artful wildness to perplex the scene;
> Grove nods at grove, each alley has a brother,
> And half the platform just reflects the other.

One can sense the stunted draper's son, his pen mightier than any purse, almost hopping with delight as each dart is dispatched; and imagine His Grace, hopping in pain and shame as they land, all his wealth and influence counting for naught.

Pope's pleasure in the science and art of gardening, and his eagerness to advertise his opinions on aesthetic sensibility, make him much cherished by gardening historians. He is seen as bringing down the curtain on the sterile excesses of the recent past, and raising it to reveal the new domain of the landscape architect. His own garden extended over no more than five acres. But his imagination helped shape much grander ambitions – among them Burlington's recreation in Chiswick of the sunlit, temple-strewn classical landscapes of Poussin and Claude Lorrain. It created that stage for William Kent, who – in Horace Walpole's phrase – 'leaped the fence and saw that all Nature was a garden'.

Kent and his noble patron had no interest in gardening from the point of view of growing things. To them the creation of the garden was a species of architecture, its purpose to realize the classical paradise. At Chiswick, the focus was on the temples and pavilions, copied from designs by Palladio, each deposited on its own eminence, to be approached by its attendant alleys. Shrubs and flower beds were distractions. What mattered was the scene. Its permitted elements were buildings, clipped hedges, standings of trees, lawns and water, as often as not surmounted by the sort of old bridge Lars Porsena of Clusium is remembered for.

All this was very fine if you happened to be an idle earl with an obsession for Italianate landscapes and a bottomless exchequer; or, indeed, a poet with clear notions of beauty and a prime site in a select London suburb to realize them. But lesser men – of substance, but without an original idea about gardening in their heads – needed practical instruction. They were not for leaping fences and embracing Nature. They had some land, and limited budgets, and they wished to know how to get the best out of both. They may well have studied John James, or – if touched by intimations of changing fashion – either Stephen Switzer's *The Nobleman, Gentleman, and Gardener's Recreation* (first published in 1715) or Batty Langley's *New Principles of Gardening* (1728).

These dusty old volumes are useful to the chronicler, as reflections of the tastes of the age. But it would be idle to pretend that either could be read today for profit or amusement. Langley's is considerably the more tedious, a Georgian equivalent to the collected works of Doctor Hessayon, without the jokes. Both Langley and Switzer adopted, to limited degrees, the new attitudes; Langley in his disapproval of topiary and ornate parterres, Switzer in his espousal of the 'twistings and twinings of Nature's lines'. And both showed a proper appreciation of the importance of cultivated grass. 'The grand front of a building should be open upon an elegant lawn or plain of grass,' instructs Langley. It should have no borders cut into it, 'for the grandeur of those beautiful carpets consists in their native plainness'. It should be adorned with beautiful statues, he says, and 'terminated in its sides' with groves. A great range of suitable classical notabilities is recommended, among them Mars, Jupiter, Venus, Apollo, the Nine Muses, Priapus, Bellona, Pytho and Vesta. But on how to produce the 'beautiful carpet' to show off the gods and goddesses to best advantage, he is largely silent.

Switzer is slightly more helpful. His tips are borrowed from John James: plenty of mould 'to keep an agreeable verdure upon all your carpet walks', plenty of 'rowling, mowing and cleansing' to keep the 'daisies, plantains, mouse-ear and other large growing herbs at bay'. He advises that the seed should be chosen from those pastures where the grass is 'naturally fine and clear' – wherever they may be found – 'otherwise you will entail a prodigious trouble on the keeping of Spiry and Benty Grass, as we commonly call it, which cuts extremely bad and scarcely ever looks handsome'.

*

We have little idea how much attention was paid to these exhortations. Switzer's and Langley's books sold well, going through numerous editions. One or other, or both, must have been found on the shelves of a goodly proportion of the country houses which, with their surrounding parks, were sprouting across the land. We know from the correspondence between William Shenstone – who created one of the most celebrated gardens of the age at his home, The Leasowes, near Birmingham – and his friend Lady Luxborough, that he lent her Langley's book. And we may guess that she derived some benefit from it when she set about beautifying the surroundings of the house to which she had been banished by her husband for allegedly immoral behaviour. In 1749 she tells Shenstone that she has stripped the upper garden of its gravel, and sown it with grass. By June it is 'tolerable green', but she is puzzled as to how to keep off 'beasts of all kinds, those in human shape chiefly'.

Shenstone himself was a curiosity: a minor poet, whose lyrics, in Johnson's words, 'trip lightly and nimbly along, without the load of any weighty meaning'; a large, clumsy, melancholic man driven by a consuming passion for his garden. The Leasowes was much visited, much admired, much described. The house, which was so neglected that the rain came straight through the roof, stood on a lawn bounded by a shrubbery and a ha-ha. Falling from it was a tangle of dingles, thick with shrubs and unkempt trees, enclosing little waterfalls and pools, cut by dark, twisting paths, and studded with a total of thirty-nine seats, on each of which the wanderer might rest and contemplate a view whose particularities were not duplicated from any other.

Johnson, standing in judgement as ever, wondered if such a creation required any great powers of mind. 'Perhaps a sullen and surly speculator,' he concludes, 'may think such performances rather the sport than the business of human reason.'

Maybe; and it is true that Shenstone ruined himself in the pursuit of his vision, and that its realization was extinguished on his death, since his family had to sell the place to pay his debts. But it is also true that his ponderings on the matter of what man might do with his surroundings bore fruit:

> Yon stream that wanders down the dale,
> The spiral wood, the winding vale
> The path which, wrought with hidden skill,
> Slow-twining scales yon distant hill,
> With fir invested – all combine
> To recommend the waving line

The verse may be insipid, but the sentiment is sound. The same may be said of many of the impressions and fancies collected in Shenstone's *Unconnected Thoughts on Gardening*. He was no great enthusiast for cultivated grass – 'a series of lawns, though ever so beautiful, may satiate and cloy unless the eye pass to them from wilder scenes'. His focus was on the relationship of Art and Nature. Addison had asserted that the value of a garden as a work of art was determined by the degree of its resemblance to nature. Shenstone had more sense. He separated the two: 'Apparent art, in its proper province, is always as important as apparent nature. They contrast agreeably; but their provinces ever should be kept distinct.'

All this wrestling with the moral dimension of Man's

responsibilities to the world given him by God may seem rather mystifying now, and most of its abundant harvest in the forms of prose and poetry lies at rest in dusty obscurity. Horace Walpole, another of those dimly remembered shadows of 18th-century literature, surveyed the age in his 'Essay on Modern Gardening'. He identified Charles Bridgeman, who died in 1738, as the first designer to escape from the tyranny of geometry; and credited him (wrongly, as it had already featured in John James's book) with the idea of the ha-ha, the sunken wall or ditch which physically separated the garden in front of the great house from the rest of the park, or the countryside beyond, without interrupting the progress of the eye across the scene. For Walpole, Kent was the hero of the age, a status in no way diminished by the fact that he was an architect and painter who worked with landscape, and had no evident interest in horticulture.

Walpole outlived both Kent and the man he nominated as Kent's successor, Capability Brown. Brown had 'set up with a few ideas of Kent', presumably acquired when both men were employed by Lord Cobham at Stowe. With Brown came a great deal more grass. Under his direction, it spread over the walls and terraces, devouring beds and shrubberies, to the very walls and doors of the mansion; so close that someone complained that the cattle could wander inside. This is not the place to grapple with the hotly debated issue of Brown's contribution to landscape gardening: whether he was a genius whose famous concern for the capabilities enabled him to create a series of uniquely English masterpieces for his aristocratic patrons; or a barbarian who laid waste to the varied inheritance of the past in order to slap on his

61

own bland formula of lake, lawn and tree clump. Brown's guiding principle was that beauty must be founded on stability and harmony, and that these indispensables were most reliably achieved through fluent, easy lines, gentle convexities and concavities. Whether consciously or not, he echoed the creed expounded by Edmund Burke in his *Philosophical Inquiry into the Origin of our Ideas of the Sublime and the Beautiful*. Smoothness, wrote Burke, is a 'quality so essential to beauty that I do not recollect anything beautiful that is not smooth'. To support this fantastic assertion, he instances the shape and texture of leaves, of mounds in gardens, of streams, of the surface of furniture, of the skin of women. 'Most people', Burke contends, 'have observed the sort of sense they have had of being swiftly drawn in an easy coach on a smooth turf with gradual ascents and declivities. This will give a better idea of the beautiful, and point out its probable cause, than almost anything else.'

Nonsense this may well be; but the notion was embraced with enthusiasm in the second half of the 18th century, and it sustained the development of the lawn as the essential canvas of the landscape garden. Capability Brown's most voluble apologist, the Reverend William Mason, composed a long and unreadable poem, 'The English Garden', glorifying among much else the master's deployment of the ha-ha, which

> . . . divides
> Yet seems not to divide the shaven lawn
> And parts it from the pasture; for if there
> Sheep feed, or dappled deer, their wandering teeth
> Will, smoothly as the scythe, the herbage shave,
> And leave a kindred verdure.

The Arcadian idyll pictured in Mason's leaden verses achieves a glimmering of reality in a series of paintings of Sir Thomas Lee's seat, Hartwell House in Buckinghamshire, which were executed by a Spaniard, Balthasar Nebot, in the late 1730s, and may now be seen at the county museum in Aylesbury. They illustrate neatly the manner in which new fashion was often grafted on to, rather than replaced, what was inherited. The elaborate topiary, grown to extraordinary heights during the previous half century, is retained. Sculpted heads in yew stand proud over sharp-edged walls of green. But instead of regarding the old rectangular parterres, they stare out over a medley of temples, statues and other cheerful stonework commissioned from James Gibb to brighten the place up.

The avenues between the high hedges are mostly of grass, as smooth as cloth. While the quality – ladies in billowing dresses with caps on their heads, gentlemen in wigs, short coats, breeches and silk stockings – stand around, the labourers labour. Two scythemen are in blouses, rough trousers and squashed black hats. One swings the double-handed cutter, the other is sharpening his blade. A lad has laid his besom on the ground and is gathering the cuttings into a basket. A girl in cap and long skirt is wielding her broom, close to a gang of mythological characters in stone, with few clothes on.

Elsewhere in the Hartwell paintings, a view of the wilderness behind the house gives glimpses of an obelisk, a temple, a turret and something resembling an igloo. Someone is pulling a roller across the grass towards a nude ancient with huge buttocks, while his fellow is gathering up more cuttings. In the distance, beyond a hedge, a flock of those useful animals dubbed the 'fleeced foragers' by William Mason are foraging. Another view shows foragers both fleeced and uddered a-nibble. In the foreground grass is being heaped by two-legged beasts of burden next to a pair of pensive gods. The lawns sweep right up to the walls of the mansion, the front door opening on to the bowling green, upon which the idle rich are at play. The green is enclosed by grass slopes, surmounted by dark barriers of evergreen.

There is another painting of Hartwell, executed twenty years later, in 1757, by a hand other than Nebot's. By now the topiary has been dug up, and the Octagonal Pond has been replaced by a lake of more 'natural' aspect. The classical statues have clearly been breeding. What has not changed are the roles. The gentry and their ladies are still sauntering about murmuring pleasantries to each other, while to one side or the other the peasantry sweat in a silence disturbed only by the swish of the scythe blade or the rasp of sharpening stone on metal. And the smooth, green turf, so soothing in appearance, so insistent in its demands, stretches away as it ever did, and does to this day.

The Hartwell paintings give an idea of how they tended the stuff. But how did they grow it? To lay down the vast expanses required by the Brownian system was a mighty undertaking. The records at Chatsworth in Derbyshire – where Brown was at work in the 1760s – tell us that, having swept away the formal terraces and parterres to the east of the house, he had the ground sown with hayseed, and then left it to its own devices. But there was at least one famous garden creator who did take a closer interest.

A visitor to Painshill, near Cobham in Surrey, wrote in 1769: 'The general scheme of Mr Hamilton's garden ... is a great Lawn, supposed 200 acres, spotted with trees and surrounded on two sides by Pleasure Grounds.' The Honourable Charles Hamilton, youngest son of the sixth Earl of Abercorn, organized the making of that lawn himself, and described how it was done in a letter to the Duke of Leinster. These were the essentials:

> Cleansing the ground thoroughly from weeds, and laying it down smooth; if any ground was very foul, I generally employed a whole year in clearing it, by ploughing it sometimes five, but at least four times, and harrowing it very much after each ploughing, first with an Ox Harrow, then with small Harrows; this harrowing brings up all the couch grass and weeds to the surface; which after every harrowing I had raked up in heaps and burned ... to make the ground even I made them plough the ridges into furrows ... then harrow across the ridges ... I set a few men to work with spades to beat about some of the loose earth.

Hamilton sowed each acre with 'six English bushels of the cleanest hayseed I could get and ten pounds of fresh Dutch clover seed'. He knew all about germination:

> If the ground was in sowing order about the beginning of August, and that month proved a wet one, I took the first opportunity I could, and sowed the grass seeds ... the moisture and warmth of that month made them grown immediately and fast enough to establish their roots before Winter, and resist the Frost.

Like Shenstone, Hamilton ploughed his own furrow in devising his pleasure grounds; and like Shenstone, he was in the grip of an unappeasable obsession; and like Shenstone, he was eventually ruined by it. But unlike the poet, he does not appear to have been a student of the theoretical aspects of the relationship between beauty, art and nature. He was a practical visionary, who took a great sweep of barren heathland and endeavoured to train it into a match for his dreams.

The lawn at Painshill came early on, in the 1730s. Samuel Richardson, author of *Clarissa* and other interminable sentimental romances, marvelled at how Hamilton 'burned the heath, spread the ashes, grew turnips, fed the sheep on the turnips', in order that 'their dung became a good manure so that a fine sward of grass is now upon the land, where it was judged by most people impossible to get any herbage'. Richardson proceeded to endow the property of his preposterous hero, Sir Charles Grandison, with the glories of Painshill:

> The park itself is remarkable for its prospects, lawns and rich-appearing trees of large growth. The gardens, vineyards etc. are beautifully laid out. The orangery is flourishing; everything indeed is that belongs to Sir Charles Grandison. Alcoves, little temples, seats are erected at differing points of view; the orchard, lawn and grass walks have sheep for gardeners; and the whole, being bounded only by sunk fences, the eye is carried into views that have no bounds.

As prose, this is awful; and the novel is surpassingly dull, sunk – in the words *of Chambers Biographical Dictionary* – by the 'prolix impeccability of its superfine hero'. But that description of the grounds of Grandison Hall is interesting, in that it may well have corresponded to the aspiration of rich country gentlemen of the mid-18th century; interesting, too, that the mowing should have been contracted out to Mason's 'fleecy foragers'.

The purpose of the great lawn at Painshill was to expose and enhance the view. Its maintenance could then be left to the foragers. Having created that view, Hamilton proceeded to create the features worthy of it. He dug a great lake with islands and ornamental bridges, built a Roman Mausoleum, a famously fanciful Turkish Tent, a Temple of Bacchus, a Hermitage which even had a hermit for a few weeks until he took to drink and was sacked. Finally Hamilton over-reached himself, with the Grotto made from tufa which he placed on the biggest of the islands in the lake. Debts closed over his head, and he was forced to sell Painshill and move to a more modest home in Bath.

But Hamilton had much to be proud of, and proud he had been. He provided horse-drawn chairs on wheels to enable casual visitors to inspect the wonders. Anyone with any pretension to involvement in the advance of taste came to Painshill. The Reverend William Gilpin, self-appointed prophet of the virtues of the Picturesque movement, descended on Painshill, and thought the Temple of Bacchus 'very happily introduced', but deplored the failings of the Great Lawn, 'too much patched by clumps and the eye disagreeably caught by white seats, bridges and the grotto'.

More significantly, Thomas Jefferson saw Painshill in 1786, when it was still not far short of its full glory. 'A boldness of design and happiness of execution', wrote Jefferson, 'attend the wonderful efforts which Art has made to rival Nature.' Could it be that Jefferson's mind retained an impression of Painshill when he ordered the laying down of lawns in the English style at his formatively celebrated Virginia estate, Monticello; that Charles Hamilton's Great Lawn glowing in the heathland of Surrey was a primary inspiration for what was to become the American passion for the cultivation of fine grass? I like to think so.

It is doubtless a symptom of the maturing of a recognizably English style of garden design that the progress of the 18th century should have seen ever more intemperate and passionate exchanges of abuse between those who had volunteered themselves as authorities on what John Evelyn, in a more innocent age, had characterized as 'the best of diversions'. Addison started it, mocking the topiarists. Pope, supreme master of invective, took up the baton, and witty Horace Walpole followed his way. But their scorn, hurtful though it must have been for their victims, can be seen as a necessary aid to growing up; and, moreover, it is amusing to read. In their footsteps, however, strode lesser men, swelled with a great sense of self-importance, deficient in wit, bursting with conceit. Poor Lancelot Brown, with his capabilities, his lakes, his sweeps of grass and soothing clumps and belts of trees, was chief target for their bile. 'Is it not singular', mused Sir William Chambers – a mediocre architect and designer and self-appointed authority on the wonders of Chinese civilization –

> that in this island the Art [of gardening] is abandoned to kitchen gardeners, well skilled in the cul-

ture of sallads, but little acquainted with the principles of Ornamental Gardening. It cannot be expected that men uneducated and doomed by their condition to waste the vigour of life in hard labour, should ever go far in so refined, so difficult a pursuit ... In England, where no appearance of Art is tolerated ... a stranger is often at a loss to know whether he is walking on a meadow, or in a pleasure ground, made and kept at a very considerable expense.

It is hardly surprising that the arrogance of these comments, and the gibe at Brown's lowly origins, should have aroused anger. Into the ring leaped Capability's staunch defender, William Mason; and Chambers retired from public controversy under a broadside directed at his anaemic, pseudo-Oriental work at what was to become Kew Gardens. But by now Gilpin's creed of the picturesque was on the march. In 1772 Gilpin published his *Observations on Several Parts of England*, illustrated with his own aquatints, in which he extolled the grandeur, variety and unpredictable wildness of untamed nature, contrasting these virtues with those of the 'embellished artificial scene', much to the latter's disadvantage.

To Gilpin's disciples – chiefly a brace of Herefordshire squires, Sir Uvedale Price and Richard Payne Knight – the soothing predictability of the Brownian formula was anathema.

> Curse on the Shrubbery's insipid scenes!
> Of tawdry fringe encircling vapid green

thundered Knight in his 'The Landscape – A Didactic Poem'. Sir Uvedale Price, in his *Essays on the Picturesque*, heaped obloquy on the legacy:

> It would be difficult to invent anything more
> wretchedly insipid than one uniform green surface
> dotted with clumps of trees and surrounded by a
> belt . . . Smoothness, verdure and undulation are the
> most characteristic beauties of a lawn, but they are
> in their nature closely allied to monotony . . . Mr
> Mason observes that that green is to the eye what
> harmony is to the ear . . . the long continuance of
> either without some relief is equally tiresome to the
> senses.

To Brown's defence came his successor as chief
designer to the great and the rich, Humphrey Repton;
possibly motivated as much by the desire to stand up
for the profession as out of loyalty to the precepts of
Capability. Repton was impatient with the intolerance of
the amateurs, and had no time for their obsession with
what he regarded as the false correlation between
gardening and painting. How they squandered their fortunes on their whims was irrelevant to the business of
making gardens. He – like Brown – had clients, who
had ideas of their own, budgets, geographically awkward
properties. To Repton, what mattered were 'congruity
of style, uniformity of character, and harmony of parts'.
His guiding light was his own excellent taste, which, for
instance, led him to banish lawns from the immediate
environs of the house and to reintroduce such novelties
as flower beds, gravel walks and conservatories.

The controversy raged on, to the close of one century
and into the next, until the protagonists ran out of brim-
stone, aged, and died, leaving the next generation to
pick out what was of lasting value, and discard the mass
of hot air. The absurdity of the row was that, when it
came to the practical application of high-flown theory,

no one had any consistent notion of what they should be doing. This impotence made the theorists very cross, apt to magnify the smallest difference in emphasis into a chasm of principle. And it is true that a corrective to the Brownian formula was probably needed, and that the reorganization of the English countryside had gone far enough. Anyway, by now great forces were at work; forces which would close the long era in which the development of the garden in England had been dictated by the inclinations and spending power of society's uppermost tier.

The Moral Lawn

The term 'lawn' is applied to that breadth of mown turf formed in front of, or extending in different directions from, the garden front of the house

JOHN CLAUDIUS LOUDON

The high and the mighty had prospered exceedingly under the House of Hanover, and a spirit of competition had grown up among the swelling ranks of the aristocracy and gentry as they acquired their country residences and set about dignifying them. Their ambitions had vaulted far beyond the provision of comfort and safety for themselves and their dependants. They aspired to mansions and estates whose scale and magnificence might be accepted by society as sound measures of their status.

Turning the pages of William Watts's *Seats of the Nobility and Gentry* (1779) and William Angus's *Seats of the Nobility* (1787) gives a sense of how well the landed aristocracy had done, and the standards of taste it had come to share. Upon the parks surrounding the porticoed piles – variously 'great and agreeable edifices', 'noble mansions', or 'great and excellently situated seats' – the mark of Capability Brown is stamped. The elements of these compositions are few, and they do not vary much. There is usually a lake, with an ornamental bridge. There are trees, in belts and clumps. There are broad gravelled drives with carriages rolling up them and dogs frolicking behind. And there is a sea of shorn grass, from which stags and their hinds stare deferentially at the great house. Close by the lord's habitation scythemen may be at work, attended by boys with baskets for removal of the cuttings. At a decent distance, beyond the ha-ha, the fleeced foragers nibble.

It is tempting to invest these old prints with a spurious quality of timelessness. They correspond with a sentimental notion of an English rural way of life held together in tranquil stability by the relationship between lord or squire and tenantry. In fact, of course, the acquisitive march of the new landed aristocracy had been rapid, self-interested, and was comparatively short-lived. Even as William Watts and William Angus were ingratiating themselves with their titled subscribers, its impetus was faltering. Capability Brown died in 1783, and although Repton strode energetically and profitably in his footsteps, the fair wind which had assisted the patrician class in helping itself to swathes of the English countryside was fast running out of puff. The war with France – with its accompanying resurrected nightmare of invasion – began in 1793, and cast its shadow for the best part of quarter of a century. In 1816, the ageing Repton, surveying the changing scene, observed sadly, 'In the last ten years, the art of landscape gardening, in common with all other arts which depend on peace and patronage, has felt the influence of war and war taxes, which operate both on the means and the inclination to cultivate the arts of peace.'

By the time Repton died, the balance of economic power had shifted decisively from the landed élite to an emergent class of men who made money by making things and selling them. The flying shuttle had come, and the spinning jenny; the steam engine and the power loom; wrought iron and cast iron. An unprecedented purchasing power was being created among people who – although they swiftly developed the urge to deploy it – were searching for the means, for someone to tell them how to do it.

Repton had managed to tack with the new breeze pretty cannily. He knew that if he continued to rely upon aristocratic patrons, the orders would dry up. Without fuss, he diversified, jettisoning most of Capability Brown's canons, and embracing a sensibly malleable version of the picturesque, calculated to appeal to a prosperous but not landed clientele. Earnestly, he assured them that he cared as much for their few acres as he had for the estates of earls and marquesses. And, being a conscientious fellow, he persuaded them sufficiently, and even himself. Almost his last work was at Ashridge in Hertfordshire, a mere eight acres, which he called 'the child of my age and my declining years'. Weary of gravel walks, broad stretches of lawn bounded by beds of flowers and shrubs – 'everywhere promiscuously mixed and repeated' – Repton flung novelty at his little patch, mingling a parterre embroidered with raised beds with a reconstructed monk's garden, a rosary, a rock garden, conservatory, cloistered walk, grotto, and much else besides; although, I'm relieved to say, he retained a lawn, dotted with shrubs.

But Repton's survival could not disguise the fact that

the sun had set on his world and his ways, and was rising on a new world, which required a new prophet. His name was John Claudius Loudon, and he was the true father of modern gardening.

Loudon, the son of a Lanarkshire farmer, was a man of many parts: designer, illustrator, writer, editor, architect, traveller, plantsman. In none of these, taken singly, was he outstanding; indeed, he hardly rose above mediocrity. His genius lay in his appreciation of the new market, and the way in which he reached out to it, combining sure instinct with an awesome thoroughness. Loudon's motivation was primarily moral rather than entrepreneurial. He was driven to deploy his almost inhuman capacity for industry by his sense of duty. His mission was to serve his fellows by educating them. To do so properly required him to acquire and digest a colossal mass of learning, and distil from it a primer of instruction. Loudon's task was to create taste, for the benefit of society. He was no charlatan. He knew his stuff, perhaps too well. Sometimes one has the sense of him almost drowning in the ocean of his erudition.

With the unstinting help of his devoted and diligent wife, Jane, and aided by a network of researchers and correspondents, Loudon organized a succession of mighty enterprises which shaped home life for the upper and middle classes in late Georgian and early Victorian Britain. He founded and edited the *Gardener's Magazine*, the *Magazine of Natural History*, the *Architectural Magazine*; compiled the *Encyclopaedia of Gardening*, the *Encyclopaedia of Plants*, the *Encyclopaedia of Cottage, Farm and Villa Architecture*, and the *Arboretum et Fruticetum Britannicum* (eight volumes classifying British trees and shrubs); wrote a

75

series of meaty works of instruction on other matters; and died exhausted and broken in health when he was sixty.

The work most characteristic of Loudon and his age is the *Suburban Gardener and Villa Companion.* On the first of its 752 densely packed pages, the tone of earnest, passionate certitude is established:

> To labour for the sake of arriving at a result, and to be successful in attaining it, are, as cause and effect, attended by a certain degree of satisfaction to the mind, however simple and rude the labour may be, and however unimportant the result obtained . . .

This is the statement of Loudon's philosophy: that the performance of a task is, of itself, good; better, by implication, than idleness. His sonorous prolixity invests a truism with the weight of a great principle. Having established it, he proceeds to grade the moral worth of outdoor activities:

> A man who plants a hedge or sows a grass plot in his garden lays a more certain foundation for enjoyment than he who builds a wall and lays down a gravel walk; and hence the enjoyment of a citizen whose recreation, at his suburban residence, consists in working in his garden must be higher in the scale than that of him who amuses himself, in the plot around his house, in shooting at a mark or playing at bowls.

An audience which knows no better is being encouraged to accept a moral distinction between enjoyment and amusement. Loudon is telling them that it is better to have something to show for the activity of their leisure – a hedge, a lawn, a flower bed – than not; and that something which grows is better than something which does not. Even more tellingly, he legitimizes and dignifies the dirtying of the fingers. Not only is it permissible to labour in the creation and improvement of a garden, it is positively good – good for the body, good for the mind, good for the character. Here, with one bound, we have left behind the world of gardens commissioned of designers by aristocrats in silks and wigs who would have fainted at the proximity of a dirty spade. The democratic garden is born, and with it a nation of gardeners.

It is easy to laugh at Loudon's Presbyterian solemnity; easier still to yawn. But by understanding what he was driving at, we may understand something about what the massed ranks of the new moneyed class did with the suburban residences sprouting forth across the kingdom. In this vast, tedious book, Loudon – by addressing himself one by one to a numbing multiplicity of domestic issues – codified a body of knowledge, and offered it up to the class which, little by little, was assuming the running of the country. It did much more than provide an answer to every question which the owning of a home could produce. In it, people could find themselves, their place. An epic social hierarchy was defined.

At the bottom of Loudon's pecking order are fourth-rate houses, built in a row 'principally for the occupation of mechanics', with appropriately modest gardens attached. Above those come third-rate properties, whose gardens may decently include fountains, a rustic thatched folly, even a Doric temple of discreet proportions. The second category belongs to 'wealthy tradesmen, professional people, and gentlemen of good fortune'; above which is placed the first rate, mansions rather than mere houses, surrounded by gardens which 'can scarcely be less than from fifty to one hundred acres'.

Once you have identified your place on the ladder, Loudon tells you all you need to know. Think of the prevailing winds, which way the dust will blow. Note the position of the sun and work out where the shade will fall. Avoid tanneries, soapworks, large manure heaps, schools and their noisy charges, churches and their bells. Be careful with the positioning of fireplaces. Attend to the matter of smoking chimneys. Lay out your laundry, larder and kitchen with regard to their interdependent functions.

For Loudon, the house and the gardens form a unity, and are complementary to each other. 'It has often struck us with surprise', he admonishes, 'that the proprietors of the finest residences in England, noblemen and gentelmen of high education and refinement in other things ... should commit the laying out of their gardens to their gardeners.' To him, house and garden had equal status; for what do you see when you look from one, but the other? And, in Loudon's view, what people of taste wanted to see from the windows of their drawing rooms was 'the smoothness of green turf'.

The lawn was Loudon's starting point, the first, essential element of the garden canvas. In the mass of designs which he devised to match the aspirations of the various social classes, the lawn was given the status of the indispensable. Loudon deployed shrubs around it, cut flower beds into it, planted trees within it, placed upon it seats, urns, statues, arches and other assorted embellishments. The Loudonian garden, whether belonging to rude mechanic or blue-blooded earl, was absolutely the creation of Man. In it, the elements of the picturesque were refined and subjugated to an extent that would have made it difficult for the Reverend William Gilpin to recognize the child as his own.

In a radical break with the past, fleeced foragers and unkempt ruminants were banished. Loudon's ideal was of

> the elegant picturesque ... stillness and consecration to Man – stillness, as being without animals or moving objects; and consecration to Man, from the mown surface greatly heightened by the circumstance of the branches of the trees reclining to the ground, which can never happen when sheep or cattle are admitted.

Having endorsed the shorn, animal-free lawn as one of the essentials of the moral garden, Loudon – unlike his predecessors – attended in exhaustive detail to the business of producing it. There was only one way: through a regime of regular, skilful scything and the thorough removal of the grass:

> For the cleaning of a lawn after a morning's mowing, every alternative swarth is to be raked with a common hayrake in such a way as to leave a breadth of two swarths for the long-handled besom. Along the centre of this space, a man starts with a flattened besom on the end of a nine-foot handle and sends all the grass he meets with a right and a left, leaving these two swarths cleanly swept. A boy or woman, with a short-handled besom, follows after and sweeps tens yards of the ridge upward and ten yards downward, thus leaving the lawn studded with heaps of grass sixty feet apart the other. This is again

basketted into the grass-cart by a man and a boy with
a couple of boards and a besom.

Followed all that? Splendid! The Loudon blueprint
enacted is a pleasure to witness:

> When this plan is followed, all is regularity; the long-
> handled besom, doing the bulk of the brushing with-
> out ever having to touch a blade of grass twice over,
> is a manly, straightforward sweeper; for the person
> stands upright as a dart, and moves forward in a line,
> swinging his arms in an even balance, furrowing the
> greensward whilst the women and boys with their
> four-foot besoms lay it in heaps.

Coming off the printed page, it sounds straightforward
and painless; and would have been, assuming you were
the one giving the orders. But imagine the appalling
drudgery of it! Picture, if you can, the scythemen, up
before dawn to be ready to catch the grass while still wet
with dew, fracturing the silence with the rasping of stone
on cutting edge, and behind the swinging of the blade,
the platoon of sweepers swishing with their besoms, and
behind them the gatherers, humping their baskets. And
remember that, even as the blades ceased their swiping,
and the baskets were being filled, the irrepressible vigour
of the stuff itself, the grass, would ensure that the whole
laborious ritual must be performed again within the week
or the fortnight.

The labour could be found – men, women and boys
ready to toil through all the hours of daylight in return
for the means to sustain life, and little more. But the
brutishness of the work did trouble Loudon, who was a
properly enlightened and – within normal limitations –
compassionate Victorian. He was aware that the workers

belonged to the same species as himself rather than to that of mules, oxen and other four-legged beasts of burden (the lawn outside his own house, in Bayswater, was even more of a burden than most, as his practice of plantings bulbs in it meant that it had to be cut with shears). Loudon noted the 'tendency to oppression' in the labour, although there is no sign that he ever considered leaving the precious greensward to its own devices.

It seems most improbable that Loudon's instructions on lawn care were widely followed, if only because of the forces and strategic precision they demanded. But on a more general level, he was instrumental in stimulating an extraordinary flowering of horticultural passion, and through the popular success of his various enterprises was able to exercise a dominant influence over the way that passion expressed itself.

One of Loudon's devotees was Samuel Barber, a neighbour of the Wordsworths at Grasmere. They mocked him for his obsession with Loudonian teaching – 'his works at the cottage begin to be too ridiculous for anything,' wrote Mary Wordsworth in 1824. Loudon himself visited Barber's garden eight years later and found it 'decidedly the most perfect thing of the kind we have ever seen'. It fulfilled his law of thematic consistency, while the poet and his entourage found its 'fairy chapel and ten thousand new things' absurd, and objected to the artificiality of its unity and its incongruity with the surrounding Lakeland and the past (for the same reason, Wordsworth detested the fashion for whitewashing cottages, which he believed should be 'received into the living principle of things'; advice which might have caused an architect to scratch his head).

Dorothy Wordsworth took a similarly dim view of those who would deposit their pallid versions of Capability Brown's formula on her beloved Lakeland. Inspecting Mr Curwen's new mansion and park on one of Windermere's islands, she found his 'shrubberies pitiful enough under the native trees ... they have made no substantial glades, it is merely a lawn with a few miserable young trees standing as if they were half-starved. There are no sheep or cattle upon these lawns. It is neither one thing nor the other – neither natural, nor wholly cultivated and artificial which it was before.'

Wordsworth took a keen interest in gardening matters. He applauded the polemics of Uvedale Price against the unnatural practices of the Brownian school. Unlike Price, however, he did not believe that picturesque beauty was an inherent quality of objects or landscape. Wordsworth was concerned with the human response, and its potential for development if properly stimulated. His own garden at Rydal Mount comprised stone-walled terraces, reached by rough stone steps planted with flowers, and thick with moss and ferns. There was a lawn, too; of the unmanicured variety, I imagine. It clearly acted on the poetic mind:

> This lawn, a carpet all alive
> With shadows flung from leaves – to strive
> In dance, amid a press
> Of sunshine, an apt emblem yields
> Of worldings revelling in the fields
> Of strenuous idleness;

Less quick the stir when tide and breeze
Encounter, and to narrow seal
Forbid a moment's rest;
The medley less when boreal lights
Glance to and fro, like aery sprites
To feats of arms address!

Yet, spite of this eager strife
This ceaseless play, the genuine life
That serves the steadfast hours
Is in the grass beneath, that grows
Unheeded, and the mute repose
Of sweetly-smelling flowers.

It may not be sublime, but there are some nice lines
in it. Other poets glanced at lawns – Arnold had one
'wet, bird-haunted', while Hardy sent a hedgehog fur-
tively across another in the 'nocturnal blackness, mothy
and warm'. But only William Empson – as far as I have
been able to discover – wrote a better poem about grass.
It is called 'Rolling the Lawn', and it is as short as it is
sardonic:

You can't beat English lawns. Our final hope
Is flat despair. Each morning therefore ere
I greet the office, through the weekday air,
Holding the Holy Roller at the slope
(The English fetish, not the Texas Pope)
Hither and thither on my toes with care
I roll ours flatter and flatter. Long, in prayer,
I grub for daisies at whose roots I grope.

Roll not the abdominal wall; the walls of Troy
Lead, since a plumb-line ordered, could destroy.
Roll rather, where no mole dare sap, the lawn;
And ne'er his tumuli shall tomb your brawn.
World, roll yourself; and bear your roller, soul,
As martyrs gridirons, when God calls the roll.

Loudon made it his business personally to inspect every serious garden in the land, among them Wordsworth's, which he rather liked. The sort of garden he disliked was represented in its most extreme form by the Earl of Shaftesbury's Gothic extravaganza at Alton Towers. This fantastic jumble of pseudo-Indian temples decorated with nonsensical hieroglyphics, castellated stables, turfed steps, imitation Stonehenge, iron-tongued, glass-eyed serpent, pagodas, gilded conservatories, corkscrew fountains, shellwork, a valley with a bridge over it but no water, and clutter of other assorted nonsense struck the Lowland Scot as being in 'excessively bad taste'. It drew from him one of his few neat morals: 'It is the work of a morbid imagination joined to the command of unlimited resources.'

In contrast to Lord Shaftesbury's fevered aberrations, the example set by the Earl of Mansfield at Kenwood was delightful to Loudon in 'the perfect unity of expression which prevails in the views obtained in every part of the grounds'. But even Kenwood was eclipsed by the gardens which aroused Loudon to an ecstasy of adoration, those attached to 'the Lawrencian Villa' in Drayton Green. These were created, at what must have been fabulous expense, by the wife of a celebrated surgeon who himself treated Loudon, and did much to relieve his discomforts. The great authority admired the husband, seems to have been a touch in love with Mrs (later Lady) Lawrence, and was clearly infatuated with her gardens. Loudon describes the charms of the twenty-eight acres in the most exhaustive detail: the rhododendrons and azaleas nestling the house, the Italian walk sentried by statues, the rustic arch furnishing a glimpse of a paddock grazed by contented cows, walls thick with entwined rose and shrub, another arch with Cupid prancing on one leg above it, fountains and urns, beds brilliant with roses, orchids and perlargoniums; and at the heart, a big, green lawn, the place from which every view presented itself. The Lawrencian miracle was that, amid such profusion, there was no confusion – the result, says Loudon, of having 'always an ample surface of naked lawn in the foreground or middle distance'.

It was all very well for Loudon, driven by his mission, and Mrs Lawrence, with her husband's abundant earnings at her disposal, to deal in these aspects of perfection. The law according to Loudon – that from the house should extend the 'extreme smoothness and high polish of the lawn' – was easy to lay down. But how were lesser mortals to observe it, without the assistance of the unpaid fleeced forager and his friends? Only by undertaking the considerable expense and trouble of having a small army of sweating labourers, plodding around the place with their scythes and besoms and baskets for hours on end, week in, week out, throughout the grass-growing season. It was a situation that cried out for one of those flashes of genius which, again and again, lit the sky of Victorian social advance. When it came, it changed the face of the English garden.

MUSINGS
FROM THE SHED
(1)

Albert's Morning March

Our home was at the end of the village, between the prongs of the fork formed by the roads to Maidenhead and to Windsor. The house was early 19th century, with later additions, architecturally undistinguished, but spacious enough for us five children, our parents, a resident grandmother and a nanny. The kitchen, where we mostly ate, was warmed by a great cream-coloured Aga, fed in those distant days with anthracite coals which rattled and clanged as they slipped from the hod into the glowing, flickering heat within. The kitchen door opened on to a brick terrace. Beyond rose a giant cedar of Lebanon. The spread of its branches and those of the big oak beside the orchard shaded and shadowed all the upper part of the garden. Beneath the cedar lay a carpet of needles, broken here and there by patches of malnourished grass fighting for existence. Beneath the oak were the daffodils, growing in long grass which was left uncut.

The lawn proper began where the sunlight was able to filter through the extremities of the canopy created by the cedar's outreaching lower branches. It extended about fifty yards, to a yew hedge which formed a break between the formal gardens and what we called The Point, where there was a concrete paddling pool – later converted to a site for bonfires – enclosed by shrubs, hazelnut trees and silver birches. There was a gap in the yew hedge, a few yards in front of which stood two slender, cigar-shaped yew bushes. These served as the goalposts in the games of football I played with two of my brothers, and Ralph, the son of our cook, who grew up with us.

Our posts were slightly to one side, allowing centres to be delivered satisfactorily from the right side only. This touchline was formed by the meandering edge of a long sweep of flower beds. The boundary between them and the road was guarded by a line of holly trees. The other touchline, as it were, was formed in part by one of the side walls of an outdoor squash court, festooned with the tentacles of a climbing rose which over the years had accounted for a host of punctured plastic footballs. Our games of cricket were played crossways, with the squash court wall acting as a barrier behind the batsman's stumps. The greenhouse was at deep gully and sustained numerous breakages.

As far as we were concerned, this garden existed for one purpose only, our sport. My mother was then, and still is, a very keen and accomplished gardener. Her perspective and ours were slightly at variance, which led to occasional difficulties. When we moved to the house, in 1952, I was a babe-at-arms, and the main lawn enclosed rectangular herbaceous borders. As we grew, these displays suffered from the impact of balls and the trampling of youthful feet. My mother decided to sacrifice them, to provide an uninterrupted sweep of grass for our games. She, reasonably, expected in return to be left in peace to her weeding; and would react with alarming fierceness if disturbed by a football whizzing past her nose, or – on one indelibly appalling occasion – landing on the back of her neck.

The influence of the lawn was at work on me at an early age, though I did not know it. To keep the grass in order we had a great and beautiful machine, a shining, green devourer of grass, designed and manufactured by engineers and craftsmen of the first excellence employed by Dennis Brothers of Guildford. My father had bought it just after the end of the Second World War. He loved to stride behind it; and after his death, when I was eight, the task was performed by Albert, who was our odd-jobman; and later by my elder brothers and, later still, by me.

I am no sort of engineer. I have no interest in, or knowledge of, the working of machines. Nor have I ever had affinity with them, except this one. Over the many years I grew to love the Dennis; that is, if the notion of loving an insensate arrangement of metal is not an absurd conceit. All right, I grew to admire it mightily, for the brilliance of its design and the marvellous reliability of its performance, and I took delight in its majestic appearance, its smell of oil and petrol and dead grass, the music it made. I became in tune with it. Without having a clue how it worked, I learned how to coax it into life when damp, or long disuse, or being overheated made it reluctant to fire. I used to scrape the accretions of dark earth from the underneath of the hard steel cutters, then rub my index finger along the burnish of the faces, imagining those edges slicing through my flesh and bone. I used to place my hand over the curve of the fuel tank, feeling it throb with the turning of the engine. I used to watch the whizzing of the leather drive belt, half persuaded that the machine had a life of its own.

The ritual at the start of mowing was akin to preparing to receive the sacrament. The Dennis was kept in a dark shed at the back of the squash court, at home on an oil-stained patch of compacted earth decorated with little clods of old grass. I would drag it out backwards, grasping the smooth steel holding bar, and the big grooved roller behind the engine would produce a grating dissonance as it scraped over the concrete standing by the door.

Outside, I would unscrew the lid to the petrol tank. It took a surprising number of turns to remove it, and one had to be careful not to drop it into the dark confusion of cogs and wheels below. The smell of the petrol as it gurgled through the funnel was delicious to me. I would turn the little bronze tap to allow it to flow, then tap a tiny knob on top of the carburettor until the metal suddenly darkened with the infusion of fuel. The starter handle was kept in a socket to one side of the roller. I would take it out, open the metal flap that protected the compression chamber, then insert it until the grooved end engaged within. A firm upward lift against the resistance would produce a throaty cough. I would depress the accelerator a touch, lift the handle again. Then would sound the music of the engine, deep and powerful. The metal beast would pulse with power and the smoke of burning oil would rise. We were ready. I would turn it towards the lawn, thrust forward the upstanding lever which engaged the cutters. As the blades whirred, the first grass would fly forwards into the curved bottom of the catching box, and the tone would swell. Forward would go the other glistening steel lever, engaging the drive mechanism; and forward the Dennis would plunge, like a war horse to the fray.

I was instructed in all this by Albert, whose affection for the mower was jealous. Albert worked on the buses, then the railways. He was small and strong, a Berkshire man with a mighty thirst for Brakspear's beer, and a mocking, laconic manner of expression which we adored. He was married to Fifi, a tiny Scottish woman who cleaned for us, polished the silver and, on occasions, made immense quantities of drop-scones which we guzzled, faces and chins shiny with melted butter. She had been 'in service' most of her life, and I don't believe thought herself any the worse than us for it. Fifi and Albert were an essential part of our extended family, a unit which, in those dim days of the 1950s and 1960s, still seemed a permanent feature of the social landscape.

Albert came one day a week – to mow, saw logs, chop down trees, cut hedges. His approach to the mowing was unvarying. He would start at the margins, cutting the fiddly bits around the shrubs and bushes and hedges. Then he would define the boundary of the main lawn with a double width of cut grass, all the way round. He would shut the Dennis down and come to the kitchen for elevenses: tea and several Woodbines. Now he was ready to bring the ceremonial to its protracted climax and conclusion. The first stripes were necessarily short, filling the curves. But as they spread towards the middle, they became longer. Back and forth he would stride, laying down those lines, pausing only to scoop up the cuttings from the box and dump them in the two-wheeled cart.

In my memory, I can still hear the regular crescendo and diminuendo of Albert's morning march, and see the spread of his imprint across our lawn. I can smell that curious sweetness of grass just cut. I can feel the soft dampness of it between my fingers, see the sparkle of the daisies against the lustre of green, recall the recurring wonder at the speed with which that glow departed and the grass became mere vegetation. Sometimes, when the truck was full, I would help push it to the compost heap, which lay against the wall beyond the big oak. At the height of the growing season, we might have to empty three or four truckloads on to the heap; and if, at the end, you turned over the harvest, you would find that it was already yellowed and greyed by decomposition. And if you pushed your hands in, you could feel the heat of decay.

By half-past twelve or so, the main lawn was finished. The Dennis, hot and smoky, would be wiped down and returned to its berth. There would be beer for Albert, and more Woodbines. Then he might take out the roto-scythe to cut the rough grass in the orchard. But, for all its usefulness, the rotoscythe had none of the magic of the Dennis, and its sound was an insistent snarl, most unmusical. [Anyhow, now we had half an hour before lunch for cricket and, with the stripes fresh and new, we might imagine ourselves at Lords or the Oval, our drives and cuts applauded by a shirt-sleeved crowd.]

Later I graduated myself. My mother had ordained that each of us had to do half-an-hour's work in the garden each day. The cultivation of flowers held no interest for me. I loathed weeding, could not stand the sensation of drying earth around my chewed fingernails. But

94

I did not mind sweeping leaves, and quite liked cutting the yew hedges and the high hornbeam which ran like a rampart above the front wall, and lopping the tops off the line of *Cupressi lelandii* which extended along the fence below the squash court; and I positively gloried in the management of giant bonfires. And I came to like mowing, without quite knowing why.

The Dennis was, in its essentials, the same model as was first marketed in the 1920s. Ours was new in 1945, and we had it for the best part of fifty years. Long after my father was dead, after the house had been sold and my mother had retreated to a lawnless town garden which we could not despoil, after the lawn which our feet had pounded for so long had been covered in new houses, after our goalposts (which had long before reached a height undefendable by the most agile goalkeeper in the world) had been uprooted, after Albert and Fifi and the nannies and that world which we and they inhabited had all gone, the great machine was still doing its duty on the cricket ground.

This was our village cricket ground, and for me is so still, after more that thirty seasons. It corresponds in almost no respect to the sentimental notions of English village cricket, of thatched pub, church spire, old stone cottages, gnarled yokels on sturdy benches. Our pavilion was – until its destruction by fire in the summer of 1999 – a primitive wooden shack devoid of all but the most elementary conveniences. It acted as a meeting point for the youth of a typical Home Counties commuter settlement, where they would smoke, drink, swear and glower, using its dark, wooden frontage as a board on which to express sexual aspirations and disappointments.

A concrete path ran between the pavilion, with its attendant tidemark of rubbish, and our outfield, a popular venue for dogs to defecate. Our square stands roughly in the middle of the recreation field – or 'rec', as it is generally known. There are football fields either side, and the field is bounded by housing developments, and a youth centre from which, on summer evenings, pound drum rolls and hideously amplified guitar chords, rehearsals for performances unlikely ever to happen.

For several years in my late twenties and early thirties (I am now a creaking veteran approaching his half century) I was captain of our Sunday team. My duties extended far beyond the mere conduct of affairs on the field – to selecting the team and massaging the egos of its disparate members, organising the making of teas and the washing up, to marking the boundary, arranging for the outfield to be cut, and preparing the pitch. I generally used the Dennis to mow the square, and an exquisitely precise Ransome Auto Certies for the strip on which we were to play. As I marched behind the mower my father, and Albert, and my brothers had marched behind, I would recapture a powerful, pungent flavour of the past. Of course, it could not be the same. There were no sinuous lines and troublesome obstructions requiring deft twirls and turns and fancy footwork; just a square, thirty yards by thirty. But enough was the same as it had been, the cleaning of the cutters, the ritual of the start, the cloud of flying grass and the smell that came with it, the division between cut and uncut, the familiar, dependable, deep-throated voice of the machine.

Then, one summer, the compression departed and

96

could not be coaxed back. The man who ran the mower repair workshop in the village said he would take the Dennis off our hands, and we saw it no more.

PART TWO

BUDDING'S
PATENT GRASS-CUTTING MACHINE.

Budding Genius

We could no more abandon the use of the mowing and go back to the scythe than we could exchange an express train for the old stage coach

Gardener's Chronicle (1872)

Had your business required you, any working day in 1800, to walk in the direction of the Severn estuary along the high grassy slopes between Minchinhampton and Stroud, you would have been kept company in the valley below you to your right by a fine bustle of industrial activity. Along the valley's floor, shut in by steep, wooded sides, twists and turns the little River Frome, its waters hastening to join the Severn. Since the early Middle Ages, when man discovered he could clothe himself more conveniently and comfortably by spinning the wool of sheep than by cutting skins off animals, the river had nourished a proud industry. The ready availability of swift-flowing clean water to drive the mill wheels and flush away the dyes, and of the prized fleeces of Cotswold sheep, combined with ease of transport to the great port of Bristol, had sustained centuries of prosperity in this place, which they called the Golden Valley. Generations of fullers, dyers, weavers and shearers had

come and gone, handing on their traditions of craftsmanship and sturdy independence of mind. They had made
the broadcloth of Gloucestershire famous throughout
Europe, so that a generous measure of the stuff was an
invariable component of Royal dowries and diplomatic
exchanges of gifts.

In this year, 1800, there was a mill every quarter of a
mile or so between Chalford and Stroud. Threaded along
the hillsides were the rows of craftsmen's cottages, a
short, steep walk from their places of work. Some of the
more modest mill owners chose to live here too, their
sturdy houses of Cotswold stone perched on precipitous
gardens. The well-to-do tended to prefer the comforts
of Stroud; others still, the magnates, commissioned their
mansions at a distance sufficient for them to avoid the
smell and the noise altogether, and left the dirty work
to their underlings.

By now many of the mills had gone over to steam
power, and no longer needed the energy of the river to
drive the wheels. Brick chimneys had sprouted, to shroud
the valley in smoke. But the water was still useful, to wash
away the dyes and to fill the new Thames–Severn canal,
which was to be the industry's highway to a sure future,
an east–west artery to bring the coal to power the new
machines and to take away the cloth to markets near and
far.

You could not have guessed, looking down into that
smoky, busy valley, that the seeds of the ruin of the industry which, for centuries, had made the Stroud area one
of the most prosperous and densely populated provincial
centres in England had already been sown. But already
the traditional heavy broadcloth was being elbowed aside

in popular affection by the lighter worsteds being produced in great volume by the much larger and more efficient mills of Yorkshire and Lancashire. Its remaining major market, making the uniforms to clad the British soldier in the campaigns against the French, had but a few years left. The introduction of the new machines, bitterly and sometimes violently opposed by the traditional craftsmen, would let loose the scourge of unemployment. But mechanization failed to enable the historically and geographically fragmented Gloucestershire mills to organize themselves to compete for the new markets.

With our convenient turn-of-the-millennium perspective, we can see it all. Look down now into the Golden Valley from Brodborough Common. The little river runs clear, unpolluted by dye, looping through a clutter of industrial estates, car parks, breeze block offices, grey corrugated warehouses. Here and there an old mill still stands, its fine old stone shaming the pre-fabricated tackiness around. One can forget that they were built, not for beauty, but to earn their keep. Now they are either empty, the looms cloaked in dust and cobwebs, or have been converted into offices. The canal, opened with such a fanfare in the 1790s, has long since been annexed by silt and bulrushes, a few stretches kept open for boys to fish for tench and roach. The roof of the canal tunnel at Sapperton – two and three-quarter miles long and one of the engineering wonders of the age – collapsed early in the 20th century and has never been repaired.

By the middle of the 19th century, the Gloucestershire woollen industry had, by and large, gone to the wall. But fifty years earlier, there was no obvious reason for anyone to suspect that this would happen. This, after all, was the Industrial Revolution. Man, through the exercise of his energy and ingenuity, was transforming his world. A new way to live had been invented, in which the potential locked up in the planet given by God would be exploited to the benefit of all. The machine was the key. Wherever there was a task which custom dictated must be discharged by hand, sooner or later a machine would be devised to do it quicker and cheaper. The social idealists believed this would liberate working people from the brutishness of their lives; though the people themselves knew better. The bosses of the mills of the Golden Valley did not much care about that aspect: profit and competition were their imperatives. They embraced the new age and put the power of their minds at its service; and the age then left them behind. It is a quirk of history that the most enduring legacy of that small burst of creative energy which attended the beginning of the end for the Gloucestershire mills should have been a machine which had no application in the cloth industry, and could do nothing to save it.

One the best preserved and most handsome of the mills of the Golden Valley is the one at Brimscombe, three miles or so upstream from Stroud on the Cirencester road. The breadth of its stone frontages, the wide slopes of slate above, seem to exhale a solid, complacent confidence. There is a plaque here, in honour of the men who founded the Thames–Severn Canal Company in 1783. The waters of the Frome slide away beneath low arches at the base of the building.

In 1790 Brimscombe Mill was bought by a prospering clothier, Joseph Lewis, who, in time, handed it down to his three sons, John, William and George. Nothing much is known of any of these Lewises, beyond the dates of their births, deaths and marriages; and the fact that one of them, John Lewis, had the gift of original thinking. In 1815, as the wars which had convulsed and exhausted Europe for a generation were coming to an end, John Lewis registered the patent of his Shearing Machine: 'My machine is so contrived that it will shear a piece of cloth in the longitudinal direction with great accuracy and rapidity, and without any intermission being necessary before the whole piece is shorn from one end to the other.'

While not ranking beside Kay's flying shuttle, Hargreaves's spinning jenny, or Cartwright's power loom, John Lewis's invention was a significant step forward. Hitherto the surplus fibres, known as nap, which were raised from the spun cloth by teasels, had been lopped off by men with shears. The skill and precision required of the shearmen had made them the best-paid section of the workforce, and the most intractable. With the arrival of John Lewis's horizontal or helical mechanical cutter, its tireless blades able to whirr away for as long as there was cloth to be napped, their day was pretty much done. Not that their passing, nor the readiness with which the machine was adopted throughout the industry, seem to have brought much benefit to the Lewises. They kept going at Brimscombe until the late 1830s, then subsided into oblivion. It was left to others to exploit the fruits of John Lewis's clever mind.

*

Mid-way between Brimscombe and Stroud was another mill, Thrupp. The name survives, attached to the village which straggles along the hill above the main road. But the mill – or, indeed, mills, for at one time there were two, a hundred yards apart – have long gone.

To Thrupp, sometime in the late 18th century, migrated a family called Ferrabee. In previous generations they had lived in Uley and Owlpen, calling themselves variously Verebee and Vereby. William, born in 1698, became a blacksmith or millwright, instead of emulating his father, a broadweaver. William's son, Edward, confirmed the family's switch away from cloth-making, working as a machine-maker and repairer. By the time he died, the Ferrabees were established at Thrupp, secure in their name and calling. The previous year, Edward's elder son, John Ferrabee, had leased Thrupp Mill with permission to convert it into an engineering factory. It became the Phoenix Ironworks, for the manufacture of machines for the clothing industry, water wheels, steam engines, agricultural machinery; indeed, almost anything made of iron.

John Ferrabee is one of the two heroes of my story. We know nothing at all about his character, his virtues or his failings. That we know anything about the bare facts of his life and antecedents is because of a Mr H. A. Randall, of Ashford in Middlesex, to whose investigative efforts I am happy to pay grateful tribute. As a youth, Mr Randall was apprenticed to the Phoenix Ironworks, and he subsequently married a niece of one of the four maiden Ferrabee aunts, who were the daughters of John Ferrabee's second son, James. According to the records deposited by Mr Randall at Stroud Museum, all four sisters lived into their nineties, sharing a house in Thrupp but never speaking to each other, and taking their tea from four teapots at the same table.

The path which brought our second hero, Edwin Beard Budding, to Thrupp is obscure. There had been Buddings (or, variously, Boddyneges, Bodings and Bodyinges) in the Stroud district since the mid-16th century. Edwin Budding was born in 1796 and baptized at Eastington, west of Stroud. He came to Thrupp in the 1820s, possibly as an employee of the Ferrabees, possibly as the lessee of his own machine shop. He defined his trade as that of machinist or mechanician, suggesting a social position somewhere between that of employer and mere craftsman.

What is sure is that John Ferrabee and Edwin Budding – factory owner and mechanical wizard – became collaborators and financial partners. That they also became friends is strongly suggested by Ferrabee's will of 1831, in which he appointed Budding his sole trustee, with the task of managing his estate until his youngest son should attain the age of 21. But we can only guess, unprofitably, about the nature of their relationship. No personal records survive, and with the two men living next door to each other and working together, there is no reason why there should have been any.

The Phoenix Ironworks was conveniently placed for the clothing mills of the Golden Valley. The Lewis brothers had their horizontal napper made there. An improved version, devised by the Lewises and their partner, William Davis – in which the horizontal blade was twisted into a spiral, to achieve continuous cutting – was also manufactured by Ferrabee. So, too, were a number of variants on the same theme, at least one of which involved a crank turned by a belt driven by a shaft.

We can assume that Budding helped make many of these machines, and saw them in action. He would have watched those spiralled cutters coming down on the furry nap, taking it off clean. And somehow the idea came to him. Was it a sudden leap, lighting up his imagination with its possibilities? Or did it grow as a seed of grass, nestled in comfortable earth until warmed into germination? I have no idea, nor any powerful preference. It is enough to imagine the scene in the ironworks: the steam, the smoke, the racket, the belch of flame, the rasp of the shovels in the heaps of coal, the clang of hammers, the hiss of the hot moulds in water, the high-pitched cries of sooty urchins and the answering softness of West Country burr; and in the midst of it, the working of the mind of a man about whom almost nothing is known, following its course.

Included in the land attached to Thrupp Mill were a number of meadows, which lay between the factory buildings and the river. It may well have been that these were occasionally scythed, and that it was this conjunction which stimulated Budding's mental leap, from grass to machine and back to grass. Whatever the spark, the idea was born and a prototype was made. There is a story that Budding and Ferrabee tested it at night, to protect it from prying eyes, either on the meadows or on the grass outside Ferrabee's house. I like to picture them hauling their brainchild out, and heaving and shoving it around by the flickering light of waving lamps, the grinding and crunching of cogs and cutters mixing with the excited mutterings of the two men as they speculated on the fortunes they would surely make.

Whatever the nature of the gestation, the child was born in 1830. Articles of agreement between Ferrabee and Budding were signed on the 18th of May of that year – 'whereas the said Budding hath invented and applied a new combination of machinery for the purpose of cropping and shearing the vegetable surface of Lawns, Grass-plots and Pleasure Grounds, constituting a machine which may be used with advantage instead of a sithe for that purpose'.

It would be wearisome to quote the articles of agreement in full. Their essence was that Ferrabee would supply the cash to enable the invention to become a marketable reality; that any profits would go to Ferrabee until his outlay was covered; and that thereafter they would be equally divided between the two. A penalty of two thousand pounds was specified should either party break the agreement. The document was witnessed by a Mr A. Merrick, of whom we know nothing for sure; although it may be more than coincidence that, a year later, Loudon's Gardener's Magazine should publish a letter extolling the virtues of the Budding machine from a 'Mr Merrick of Cirencester'.

The patent was obtained in October 1830. The accompanying specification describes the machine in turgid and indigestible detail, a great block of print clogged with references to pinions, drives, cylinders, toothed wheels, brass rings, spiral cutters, bevelled steel plates, chase mortices, ratchet wheels and the like. But in the two accompanying diagrams – of the mower from the side and from above – the beauty and brilliance of

Budding's concept burst forth. There, in every essential, is the cylinder mower as it exists today. There are the elegant upward curve and flattening of the guiding handles, the roller which controls the cut; and there are the six tempered cutters, arranged in agreeable harmonious congruity around the central axis. And you think: yes, there is the mower in my shed, my mower. In that recognition is the recognition of the genius of Budding.

In the specification which accompanied the patent, it is perhaps possible to discern an echo of the voice of the inventor, as he advances its merits: 'It is advisable to employ the machine when the grass or vegetable is dry. Grass growing in the shade, too weak to stand against the scythe to be cut, may be cut by my machine as closely as required, and the eyes will never be offended by those circular scars, inequalities and bare places, so commonly made by the best mowers with the scythe, and which continue visible for several days. Country gentlemen may find in using my machine themselves an amusing, useful and healthy exercise.'

It is through that last sentiment – tentatively and awkwardly expressed – that Edwin Budding lifted the curtain on the new world made possibly by his cleverness. In the old world, grass was cut by a hired hand, in damp weather or at dewy dawn, with an implement which by its nature militated against the achievement of smoothness and evenness of texture; or it was not cut at all. Suddenly we have a vision: in which the grass may be cut when the sun is shining, at a time of day when a reasonable person might think of being outside for recreation, with an implement requiring neither great skill nor long practice; in which the care of grass becomes the duty and pleasure of its owner, rather than one more task for the paid labourer; and therefore one in which the lawn is not just an adornment of the domains of the privileged few, but a source of pleasure for the many. What Budding and his friend had done, in that workshop and on those unkempt meadows by the Frome, was to create something which might bring within the common grasp the beauty and beneficent quality of cultivated grass. They made possible a small, peaceful revolution which, in a small, peaceful way altered the face of our land.

Budding plays no further active part in the story. But he deserves a decent farewell, for there is a stirring romance in the fragments of his life, the manner in which he emerged from his natural obscurity, made his mark, and returned to the shadows. It is not known how long he remained at Thrupp, nor what caused the parting of the ways with Ferrabee. There is no evidence that his great invention made much material difference to his life. It may well be that the comparatively comfortable estate he left his widow was nourished by the proceeds from another of his inventions: an adjustable spanner identical in all essentials to the one in use today, which was made in large numbers by Ferrabee and was still being advertised by the family business many years later.

Its creator moved to Dursley, not far away, but far enough, perhaps, to hint at a cooling in the relationship with Ferrabee. On the other hand, some sort of co-operation persisted, for at the Great Exhibition of 1851 the company advertised a later Budding patent, an agricultural chaff-cutter which employed the same spiral principle as the mower. While at Dursley, Budding associated professionally with George Lister, whose second son was to found the celebrated engineering works with which the town is identified to this day. George Lister had come to Dursley from Yorkshire in 1817, setting up in business as a maker of cards, implements used to sort out and line up fibres before spinning. Together with Lister, Budding developed a new carding machine, which provoked unrest among manual workers fearful for their jobs. There is a record of Budding – an improbable candidate as industrial tyrant – being placed under police protection.

He lived in a modest, wisteria-clad cottage on the way to Stinchcombe Hill, and died there in 1846, at the age of 50. A later George Lister, in some notes written in 1952, recalled attending a school run by Budding's daughters. According to these records, Budding's widow, Elizabeth, survived him until 1874. There is no hint of what brought Budding to his grave. He lies in the churchyard in Dursley, in the heart of a town which thrived on the reputation of its great engineering works, and is now sadly decayed. We cannot know if Budding followed the fortunes of his great gift to the nation. If so, let us hope that in the year of his death, he read with pride a note in the Gardener's Chronicle from one who signed himself 'Ortolano' and who had seen the Budding machine at work:

> 'On a visit to a suburban residence . . . it appeared to answer perfectly . . . it is scarcely possible for any lawn to look more smoothly and nicely . . . it would be impossible to keep the lawn in so condition by the scythe'.

If there was a rift between Budding and John Ferrabee, it seems unlikely that it sprang from disputes over how the proceeds from the lawnmower should be divided; for the spoils were pretty meagre. In 1832 Ferrabee did issue a production licence to the agricultural machinery company, J.R. and A. Ransome of Ipswich. In time, of course, the name of Ransome was to become almost synonymous with mowing excellence. But the firm's founding fathers were hardly swift in exploiting the potential of Budding's invention. By the time its creator died, they had sold no more than 1200 of the machines, a rate of about eighty a year. Orders from the Phoenix Ironworks may have been more brisk, but the mower proved no goldmine.

John Ferrabee died in 1853, the business being passed to his sons James and Henry. The brothers went their separate ways two years later, with James retaining the ironworks, and continuing to market 'Budding's machine'. In 1858, however, it had become Ferrabee's Improved Lawn Mowing Machine. In advancing its claims in an advertising leaflet on that year. James Ferrabee asserted – with a certain air of desperation – that: 'Notwithstanding the pretensions of others, who have done little else but imitate, all the most valuable improvements in Mowing Machines have originated with Mssrs Ferrabee; their long practical experience has enabled them to avoid change without advantage, and to reject useless novelties'. The sad fact, which, in attempting to refute he implicitly acknowledged, was that Ferrabee had been left behind. The rich harvest from the act of genius which his father had helped nourish would be gathered in by others.

In 1863 James Ferrabee left the Phoenix site, and moved upstream to Brimscombe, where he began making cloth as well as continuing with some machine production. But diversification failed to provide any relief from the pressure exercised by his competitors. Ferrabee's fortunes declined. In 1872 he wrote to his son to caution him against drinking 'stimulants of any kind beyond a glass or two of beer', and informing him that from the beginning of the year 'you will be on your own resources because of the need to observe the strictest economy at home and in every other way'. He died three years later, and was honoured by some affecting lines in the local newspaper:

> 'Science hath lost a favoured son,
> His task complete, his laurels won;
> He rests from toil, from care he's free
> And wreathed by fame is Ferrabee'.

As for the Phoenix site, it was eventually occupied by another engineering company, George Waller and Sons, makers of pumps and other precisely engineered machines. This grew and prospered, and later declined, and eventually succumbed to the fate which has over-taken once proud centres of mechanical skill through the land. These days, the name Phoenix survives, attached to a trading estate between the swift little river and the weedy canal. The place of the old ironworks is taken by a publishing house. Of the mill and the workshops, that is no trace. All is submerged beneath the tarmac of the carparks, and the grey metal warehouses with green roofs.

But the place of this place in our history, and the men

who made it that, are not wholly forgotten. Over the door of the publishing house is a plaque: 'Here in 1830 John Ferrabee manufactured the first lawn mower to the design of Edwin Budding'.

The Budding's Flowering

Grass is at once the symbol of our life and the emblem of our mortality . . . the carpet of the infant becomes the blanket of the dead

J. J. INGALLS

In those early days, John Ferrabee must have had high hopes of realizing high ambitions for his friend's invention. Almost at once, he brought off what must have seemed a considerable marketing coup, by enlisting the warm support of the pre-eminent gardening authority of the day. Within a year of the mower's registration, Loudon's *Gardener's Magazine* carried a tribute to it from Mr Curtis, head gardener at the Zoological Gardens in London, which was based on a four-month trial. Mr Curtis was reported to be 'entirely satisfied' with his Budding, finding that 'with two men, one to draw and one to push, it does as much work as six or eight men with scythes and brooms; not only in mowing but in sweeping up and lifting into a box, performing the whole so perfectly so as not to leave a mark of any kind behind'.

Loudon was impressively alert to the machine's potential, albeit typically sententious in discussing its merits. 'It promises', he wrote in his notes in the September

1831 issue of the magazine, 'to be one of the greatest boons that science has conferred upon the working gardener in our time.' One of its chief attributes – that it worked best when the grass was dry – was seen by Loudon as having an important moral dimension:

> When it is used, men cannot be set to work at it very early in the morning or late in the evening. In this emancipation we rejoice. The nearer that all labourers are brought to a level, in point of severity as well as skill, the better, for various reasons; and the progress of improvement has decidedly this tendency.

Loudon loses no time in appropriating Budding's concept in the name of that ideal of human advance so characteristic of his age. There is no thought in his head that the labourer should labour less; that, having cast aside his scythe, he should be allowed to lean against a gatepost and have a smoke. His emancipation is to be able to toil when the sun is up, rather than during hours designated by the Creator for rest; to be able to exchange scythe time for fork time or spade time. It was not the labour force which was emancipated, but productivity. Extra capacity simply made it possible for more to be done, in gardening just as in factories. As for Budding's suggestion that gentlemen – such as Loudon – might care to try it for themselves, the great arbiter seems to have preferred to ignore it.

Loudon's mission was to map out the direction that liberated ambition should take. He saw the Budding as another means to empower the swelling ranks of those with money and leisure. But in the confidence of his prediction – 'we are much mistaken if it does not soon come into use in all large grounds' – he misjudged. Even though, a few months later, the *Gardener's Magazine* carried a much longer article about the Budding, complete with detailed instructions on how to operate it, and drawings illustrating its inner workings, there is no evidence of widespread interest in it. Apart from the encomium offered by Mr Merrick of Cirencester, there is no mention of it in the magazine's pages for five years, until November 1837, when Mr Samuel Taylor, of Stoke-Ferry in Norfolk, wrote in praise of 'that very ingenious contrivance, Budding's grass-cutter'.

Mr Taylor's letter offers some clues as to why the mower had failed to ignite public enthusiasm. He himself deplores the ignorance of others – 'the use and value of this instrument do not appear to be so well understood as they deserve to be' – before exposing the defective state of his own knowledge by asserting that 'the wetter the grass the better it seems to cut'; and, further, that the earth left by the worms 'seems to put an edge on the knives rather than to injure them'. Mr Taylor concludes his testimonial by offering the improbable hope that 'I shall be the means of selling Mr Budding several machines', and by recording that 'my garden abuts the turnpike road and I am seen at work by everyone passing'.

There is no record of what sort of spectacle he presented as he manhandled his Budding through the soaking grass. But it is unlikely that he would have resembled at all closely the figure in John Ferrabee's original advertising material, who was supposed to reinforce the contention that this was an amusing exercise for the gentry. This nattily whiskered beau ideal, in top hat, tail coat, tight white trousers and boots, is seen in effortless control of his Budding against an Arcadian backdrop, for all the world as if the machine was powering itself. The reality, a foretaste of the eternal chasm between aspiration and achievement in grass cultivation, was very different.

In fact, the mower made strenuous physical demands of its operator. Being made of cast iron, it was extremely heavy. The clutch had to be held in position to obtain the drive, while a firm downward and forward pressure had to be maintained to keep it moving and cutting. In the early models, a small iron roller was placed between the cutters and the big roller at the back, which made it difficult to control the height of the cut, the blades tending to alternate between revolving in the air above the grass and scalping it.

Advertising material issued by Ransomes in the 1830s reflects some of the drawbacks of the new technology. In one illustration, the first cousin of Ferrabee's top-hatted country gent is sauntering behind an apparently self-propelled Budding. But in another, an unmistakeable member of the labouring class is bent into his machine in a pose eloquent of effort, his back leg stretched out behind as if he were a muleteer trying to shift an obstinate beast. On the far side of the considerable expanse of grass which he is endeavouring to cut stands a mansion in which the quality are doubtless diverting themselves without a thought of the fun to be had from changing places with him. The accompanying text proclaims that 'persons unpractised in the art of Mowing' are now able to 'cut Lawns, Pleasure Grounds and Bowling Greens with ease'. But there is no evidence of a rush to test the assertion.

The general state of enlightenment is probably

reflected with reasonable accuracy in Cobbett's *The English Gardener*. Having delivered himself of a mass of common sense on a great range of horticultural matters, Cobbett considered briefly the matter of grass. It is evident from the edition published in 1833 that he had never heard of Budding or his contraption; though of the lawn – or grass-plat as he calls it in his old-fashioned way – he clearly thinks highly. Cobbett has no time for sowing seed; cut the turf from some 'very anciently and closely-pressed pasture where the herbage is fine' is his counsel. If anything, he is sentimental about the use of the scythe: 'A good short-grass mower is a really able workman; and if the plat have a good bottom, he will leave it very nearly as smooth and as even as the piece of green cloth which covers the table on which I am writing.' While Cobbett is properly appreciative of the charms of turf – 'grass-plats are the greatest beauties of pleasure grounds if well-managed' – he has a warning: 'If, however, you do not resolve to have the thing done in this manner, it is much better not to attempt it at all.' Then he grumbles: 'The decay of gardening in England in this respect is quite surprising.'

But perhaps not so surprising. The Georgian age, of grand houses in grand parks kept tidy by armies of retainers, had exhausted itself. The social upheaval attending the birth pangs of an industrial society had shaken and loosened the grip of the landed aristocracy. Many of the grand old estates had become economically too much for their owners, and had either been broken up or had fallen into the hands of people with a more hard-headed idea of what constituted necessary expenditure. The march of the new moneyed classes was only just gathering momentum, and the gardening pioneers were tending to concentrate their energies on the vast range of new species of tree, shrub and flower, or on novelties, such as the heated glasshouse. Loudon, directing operations, was attempting to organize the disparate elements into a discipline, and it took time for his voice to impress itself upon his audience.

Loudon marketed his guiding principles under the sonorous but meaningless label 'gardenesque', which he employed to legitimize anything which took his fancy. Philosophically he advocated the primacy of art over nature, the garden as an expression of man's ingenuity and energy. In practice, this meant a tremendous enthusiasm for plants from abroad, and for technical innovation. He occasionally made a fool of himself: one vision of progress was of a series of gigantic glass palaces, each enclosing a sample eco-system from a distant land, complete with birds, plants and animals, and a handful of appropriate natives 'habited in their particular costumes', to keep the place in order.

Loudon is seen by the majority of authorities as the father of modern gardening, an inspired and indefatigable tutor who opened a generation's eyes to the joys of this divinely approved pastime; and by a handful of sceptics as the corrupter of an art previously practised by men of refinement into an amusement for the vulgar middle classes, encouraging through his own lack or suppression of higher sensibility what was to become the Victorian mania for exotic species, garish colours, dreary and fussy arrangements of shrubberies and flower beds, and assorted other crimes of tastelessness.

All that concerns my story is that Loudon never

deviated from his allegiance to the lawn. In every one of the countless models he produced – whether for pluto-crat, aristocrat or humble professional, whatever vari-ation he permitted in the provision of bloom, shrub or tree – the lawn was the indispensable. But this status was accompanied by responsibilities. It was by no means enough just to lay the lawn down. The owner had a duty to keep his grass, like his workers, healthy:

> It is a great mistake to suppose that anything is gained in the way of economy, by suffering the grass of lawns to grow long before mowing in order to save the expense of once or twice mowing during the season; for, in proportion as the grass is allowed to grow long before mowing, in the same proportion are the roots strengthened and enabled to send up still longer leaves and stems; whereas, if the lawn were kept short for two or three years in succession, the plants of grass would become so weak that not one half the mowing usually required for even slovenly kept lawns would be necessary, and the turf would be much finer and neater in appearance.

Working one's way through this doughy prose, one wonders fleetingly if the great fount of wisdom talked like that. The opinion he expresses – that grass infrequently mown grows faster than grass frequently mown – is non-sense. But that is beside the point. Loudon's purpose is to set out one of the gardener's obligations. To have a garden is not an amusement (although there is nothing actually wrong in enjoying it). It is to undertake a res-ponsibility approved by society. Failure to discharge it properly, it is implied, will be interpreted by society as a symptom of unfitness to belong. A man may as properly have a fork or a spade in his hand as a Bible. But should he cast aside his implement before the job is done, he will be judged.

That homily is quoted approvingly by his wife, Jane. She, having accompanied him on his endless horticultural pilgrimages, acted as his secretary and amanuensis, cared for him during his bouts of ill-health, and finally buried him, continued with his mission to inform. Mrs Loudon's books – among them, *Gardening for Ladies* and *The Ladies' Companion to the Flower Garden* – were immensely popular, and, by sanctioning gardening as a suitable pastime for women, were in their way as influential as his.

On the place of the lawn, her sentiments were identical with those of him whom she continued to regard as the source of truth: 'The chief beauties of the lawn', she parrots, 'are the uniformity of its surface and uniformity in the kinds of grass which cover it and produce a uniform tone of green . . . Everyone must have felt the relief afforded to the eye by a broad strip of lawn, bordered by trees and shrubs not in a formal line on each side, but running into numerous projections and recesses.' Mowing, she intones, must be done very frequently, certainly every fortnight, although she concedes that 'it is an operation which a lady cannot easily perform for herself; unless, indeed, she has the strength to use one of Budding's machines'.

Loudon died in 1843. The records are silent as to whether he ever mowed his own lawn with his Budding. I am inclined to doubt it, since, in general, he showed no inclination to extend his pleasure in lecturing the labourer into a readiness to take his place.

*

During the early Victorian years, the cause of the mechanical grass-cutter advanced but slowly. One can only guess at the level of sales. As we have seen, Ransomes were selling no more than eighty a year. Ferrabee's probably exceeded that volume, since in 1858 James Ferrabee announced – with what degree of accuracy we cannot be sure – that total sales of the Budding had passed seven thousand. Modified versions of the Budding remained the standard choice throughout these years. But horizons were expanding. The year before Loudon's death, an engineer from Arbroath, Alexander Shanks, registered the patent for his grass-cutting machine. Although the operation of its cutters followed the Budding principle, Shanks's mower was much bigger (the prototype was 27 inches wide, compared with Budding's 16 inches), and was designed to be pulled rather than pushed.

The man who commissioned it, Mr Lindsey Carnegie of Kimblethmont, was thrilled:

> Its success surpasses my expectations. The lawn of two and a half acres is now cut, the grass swept up and the ground effectually rolled by my gardener, assisted by the pony, in two-and-a-half hours, and the execution leaves nothing to be desired. Where the ground is much fugged [i.e. the grass left long], a surface is produced very similar to velvet.

Shanks's second model was 42 inches wide, and it cost around £20 (a hefty sum, not much less that the annual stipend of some ill-favoured country curates). It was clearly much better suited to large gardens than the Budding, and the fact that it was drawn made it less likely to chew up the ground.

Shanks and Sons evidently did good business. By the

late 1840s they were advertising models between 15 and 42 inches, with a selection of testimonials from notable clients – including Lord Kinnaird, who recorded that his Shanks, propelled by a man, a pony and a woman (in that order) could cut and tidy an area of two and a half acres in seven hours, which previously had kept four scythemen and three women occupied for three days. Shanks's machines were being hauled round the new Royal Botanic Gardens at Kew, and Regent's Park, the horses being equipped with made-to-measure leather boots to minimize the damage to the turf. The 42-incher was shown at the Great Exhibition, and a few years later was displayed in Paris, where Napoleon III ordered one.

Other manufacturers entered the fray, among them Wood and Sons of Banbury, Green of Leeds, and Samuelson, also of Banbury. All their mowers were, in essence, Buddings. But the general advance in the making of machine tools opened the way to improvements. Thomas Green solved one basic problem with the Budding design, by placing a small wooden roller in front of the cutting cylinder, which provided stability and restrained the tendency of the blades to dig rather than cut. Another serious social failing of the Budding was the atrocious racket it made as its gears and cogs and shafts ground together. Green solved this, too, introducing in 1859 the magnificently named Silens Messor (the 'Silent Reaper'). This made use of a chain drive (as on a bicycle) in which a toothed wheel at the side of the rear roller revolved a chain, which in turn drove a much smaller wheel attached to the cutters.

Down at the Phoenix Ironworks, James Ferrabee, doubtless infuriated by the way others were cashing in on his family heirloom, strove to regain the market initiative. He promiscuously adopted modifications developed elsewhere, and claimed them as his own. His Improved Mowing Machine, introduced in the late 1850s, had the smaller roller placed in front of the cutting cylinder, which – with the fixed blade and adjusting mechanism – could all be detached for repair and cleaning. A few years later came Ferrabee's Noiseless Lawn Mower, chain-driven like Green's Silens Messor. He also sought to undercut his rivals. His 12-inch machine – with which, he claimed, a 'strong boy' could cut five hundred square yards in an hour – retailed at five pounds fifteen shillings, compared with six pounds ten shillings for Ransomes's equivalent.

By the 1860s the number of lawn enthusiasts was clearly multiplying rapidly. The swift expansion in mower manufacture, and the extravagance of the boasting by the companies involved, caused difficulties for the consumer. For enlightenment they were able to turn to the publication that soon established itself as a crucial element in the flowering of gardening as a pastime for the masses. This was the *Gardener's Chronicle*, the weekly newspaper introduced in 1841 as a record of 'everything that bears upon horticulture or garden botany'. Founded by the devoted apple-grower and horticulturist John Lindley, and Joseph Paxton, the gardening colossus of the Victorian Age, the *Chronicle* remains an amazing testimonial to the depth and power of the passion that had been awoken in the British. The paper fulfilled its promise. Anything and everything to do with the pursuit was gathered in, examined by expert eyes, commented on, rejected, endorsed. For anyone with an opinion or an experience nourished by the garden, it was the only vehicle for expression.

Thus, when Mr Pettigrew of Cheetham-Hill, Manchester, had trouble with his Budding, the readers of the *Chronicle* knew about it: 'The wooden roller of the unimproved implement was most objectionable', Mr Pettigrew complained in 1852, 'as it caused the machine to be difficult to hold and draw.' But he still loved it: 'I am enamoured of the mowing machine, though I know many gardeners prefer the scythe. At this place it takes four men with scythes thirty-one hours to cut our grass – 124 hours of mowing. Two men with a machine take thirty-five hours – i.e. seventy hours.'

Three years later there was a cry of anguish: 'Can anyone inform me which is the very best mowing machine? For some years I have used a Budding ... Samuelson's will not answer.' Back came the answer from another correspondent: that Samuelson's Improved Budding would answer perfectly well – if the operator would remember to take the travelling wheels off it.

In the issue of 15 June 1857, there was a letter from James Ferrabee at the Phoenix Ironworks, protesting plaintively that no one had told him about a recent trial of mowing machines at Chiswick Gardens. The following year the *Chronicle* supervised another test, to which Ferrabee was invited; although in hindsight he probably wished he had missed that one, too. Four machines were ranged against each other, supplied by Green, Shanks, Ferrabee and Deane. They were given six-and-a-half-minutes to perform, and were assessed according to the area cut, the quality of the cut, the excellence or otherwise of construction, and the ease of manoeuvre. The

Green machine was the clear winner, mowing a greater area (1,600 square feet) more smoothly than any other. Although Ferrabee's Budding cut the second biggest expanse (1,503 square feet) the quality of the work was judged the worst. In the overall table published in the paper, Green was top, Shanks second and Ferrabee third. The Deane machine was considered a general failure on every count.

James Ferrabee's reaction to this humiliation can only be guessed at. That of Alexander Shanks was conveyed in a later issue of the *Chronicle*. He described the contest as 'purely ridiculous', and stoutly maintained that 'our machine stands second to none'. These trials of mechanical strength were popular with the public, but less so with the manufacturers – unless they happened to win, in which case the triumph was noised abroad at maximum volume. Some years later the *Chronicle* published a report alleging dissatisfaction among the members of the All-England Croquet Club with the quality of the playing surface provided by its Green mower, which was compared most unfavourably with a new-fangled American import, the Archimedean. The immediate response of Thomas Green and his son was to hasten from Leeds with their own 18-incher and proceed to cut the Club's lawn 'rapidly, cleanly and evenly'.

The manufacturers were jealous of their reputations, the *Chronicle*'s correspondents increasingly confident in their own judgements. Mr Conaty of Tadcaster was pleased with his Green, which was capable of cutting four to five acres of grass a day drawn by a 'steady, active pony'. His Ferrabee 30-incher, though, 'played strange pranks on uneven ground or crossing gravel paths, answering the two-fold purpose of paving spade and culti-vator'. To Mr Radcliffe of Okford Fitzpaine, the lawn produced by the Reverend R. Price in partnership with his 10-inch Green verged on the miraculous, 'being smooth enough for billiards'. Such a toy suited Mr Price, but for the man with wide open spaces to keep in trim – such as Thomas Challis, head gardener at Wilton House – the Shanks 42-inch reigned supreme. His seventeen-year-old machine, he informed the *Chronicle* in 1868, cut the fifty acres of lawn each fortnight. He had, he said, 'discontinued the use of the scythe altogether'.

Although the occasional sentimentalist would pipe up on behalf of the scythe, there was overwhelming recog-nition that, in the context of cultivated grass, its day was done. The editor of the *Gardener's Chronicle*, writing in 1870, observed:

> Twenty years ago mowing machines were but coming into notice and but little believed in. Now they are all but universal, and the time-honoured scythe (to learn the use of which was such a severe trial to many a young gardener) is rapidly disappearing. What a revolution! What a saving of time! And how much more healthy are our lawns kept under the new than the old system.

These remarks were occasioned by the arrival on the scene of that American intruder to which Thomas Green took such exception. The novelty of the Archimedean was that, with a cutter shaped like a screw, it scattered the cuttings on the ground rather than depositing them in a box. A warm debate ensued over its virtues and failings. Some held that it had the advantage over machines of the traditional British design, because it could cut when the grass was long and wet. Others objected to the unsightliness of the strewn cuttings, and the ribbing effect left by the screw. To and fro the rival bands of supporters batted their experiences and prejudices, until the editors closed the matter, ruling that the home-grown tradition had the edge in quality of finish, while the newcomer had its uses in gardens where high quality was not the first consideration.

By that year, 1870, Ferrabee had fallen by the wayside, and the market was dominated by Ransomes, Green and Shanks, with the Ipswich firm – Ransomes, Sims and Head, to give it its full name – leading the way. In 1867 Ransomes had introduced its 'Automaton' range, in which the use of steel, improved gearing, and ball bearings provided a markedly superior performance in terms of noise, durability, finish and ease of use. By the end of the decade more than three thousand Automatons had been sold, ranging from the 10-inch model 'for a lady or lad', to the 20-incher requiring a man and a boy. Five years later sales had reached ten thousand, and a new factory had been opened in Ipswich devoted exclusively to meeting the booming demand. By then Ransomes had inaugurated the Little Gem, available in 6-inch and 8-inch widths, which soon rivalled the Automaton in popularity.

Apart from the Archimedean screw, the other important design advance of this period came from Manchester, where two engineers, Frederick Follows and John Bate, patented a mower which dispensed with the back roller, the cutters being driven by two side wheels. This made the machine much lighter, and the other companies soon appropriated the innovation.

It would be irksome to record the expansion of the motor mower industry in detail. It is enough to state that by, say, 1873 – the year Livingstone's body was brought back from Africa to be buried at Westminster Abbey – the industry had come of age, able to satisfy any reasonable demand. There was a reliable model for every case: the lady whose idea of amusement was to trip across the grass leaving a 6-inch-wide strip behind her; the gentleman with a serious sense of the benefits to self and society in the well-tempered lawn; the head gardener with a sweeping sward and a master who demanded perfection; the groundsman at a cricket ground; the secretary of a croquet or lawn tennis club. And the keenness of the competition had the customary effect on prices. The cost of the basic 16-inch cylinder machine hardly changed in the second half of the 19th century. The Ferrabee model of 1848 cost six pounds ten shillings, the Ransomes New Automaton of 1888 the same.

Poor John Ferrabee! Poor Edwin Budding! Their vision and resourcefulness had made all this possible, yet no one remembered them. Could James Ferrabee have seen the first page of Ransomes catalogue of 1888, he must have groaned in envious despair:

> Ransomes Lawn Mowers. In constant use in the Gardens of Her Most Gracious Majesty the Queen, HRH the Prince of Wales, HRH the Duke of Edinburgh, HRH the Duke of Connaught, the Royal Horticultural Society, the Royal Botanic Society . . . His Grace the Duke of Northumberland . . . the Most Honourable the Marquis of Downshire . . . the Earl of Egmont . . . Lord Brabazon . . . Lady Jane Taylor . . . Madame Patti . . .

And so it goes on, the roll call of the highborn, the rich, the successful, the celebrated – united by a willingness to associate their distinguished names with that of a humble engineering company grown fat by making something which, in its essentials, was still the same machine as had been pushed around those meadows by the Frome back in the days when Victoria was no more than a princess. It is to be hoped that the grass in Stroud cemetery – where James Ferrabee was laid to rest – was not kept in order by a Ransome!

GREEN'S PATENT SILENS MESSOR,

OR

NOISELESS LAWN MOWING, ROLLING, AND COLLECTING MACHINES.

By Special Appointment, Sole Manufacturer

To Her Most Gracious Majesty the Queen.

Improved Patent Lawn Mower for 1865, as recommended by the judges of the Royal Horticultural Society's show held July 20th, 1864.

The Glory of the Garden

They were the smoothest lawns in the world, stretching down to the liquid slowness and making, where the water touched them, a line as even as the rim of a champagne glass

HENRY JAMES

During the first twenty years of Queen Victoria's reign, the balance of gardening power shifted decisively from the commissioning élite to the more-or-less actively involved, property-owning middle classes – where, broadly speaking, it has remained ever since. Of course, great men with resources to match continued to engage the successors of Brown and Repton to aggrandize the environs of their great homes. Paxton at Chatsworth, Barron at Elvaston Castle, Barry and Fleming at Trentham organized gardens on the grandest scale, whose common purpose, whatever the differences in realization, was to display the brilliance and originality of the mind of man, rather than to refine and harmonize what nature had already provided. Lesser mortals marvelled at the boldness of these heroic designs, but generally did not take them home with them. For their own suburban grounds, they tended to seek advice from more modest and congenial sources.

133

The day of the professional gardening writer, ushered in by Mr and Mrs Loudon, had come to stay. No longer was the subject left – as it had been in the 18th century – to poets and belletrists such as Pope and Walpole, or to wealthy amateurs and choleric controversialists like Uvedale Price and Richard Payne Knight; or, indeed, to axe-grinders and self-appointed arbiters of taste such as Thomas Whately and William Mason. What the new purchasing public wanted was not flowery theorizing spiced with Augustan conceits, but solid, practical advice on what to do with their gardens: how to lay them out, what to grow, how to grow it, where to obtain the recommended plants, how to keep it all in order, how much it was all going to cost. The new authorities had to come down from the heights along which their literary predecessors had ranged, to take up a position just slightly elevated above the heads of their audience, akin to that of parsons in pulpits. Unlike men of the cloth, their advice had to be sound and comprehensible, for they had to please their congregations or perish. But a strong moral element to the sermonizing was still obligatory.

One of the absolutes in the moral code of gardening was the lawn. Its place was energetically promoted by James Shirley Hibberd, probably the most influential of Loudon's successors. Hibberd was a sailor's son, born in Stepney, later resident in Stoke Newington and Muswell Hill. As well as editing two periodicals, the *Floral World* and a resuscitated *Gardener's Magazine*, he produced a clutch of books and monographs, some – such as *Profitable Gardening*, *The Amateur's Rose Book* and *The Amateur's Greenhouse* – unpretentiously practical, others – among them *The Ivy*, *The Fern Garden* and *Brambles and Bay Leaves* – more esoteric. Hibberd's range of interest was far-flung, his curiosity boundless. But the constant at the heart of whatever garden he was constructing, in reality or in his mind, was the lawn.

He presented his articles of faith in *The Town Gardener* of 1859. 'A piece of bright green turf and a goodly show of evergreen shrubs are the very essential features of a garden, whatever its size or situation,' he wrote. Almost twenty years later, in *The Amateur's Flower Garden*, he was urging 'the greatest possible breadth of well-kept turf consistent with the area enclosed for the purposes of pleasure'. His stated purpose, in the earlier book, was to assist the metropolitan to 'insure a patch of bright green grass in the very centre of London or any other great and smoky city'; to have for himself a version of the gardens of the Inner and Middle Temple, where 'Mssrs Dale and Broome teach a daily lesson all the year round to all those who are willing to learn the alphabet of town gardening.' (This, we understand, is a man who knows gardeners by name, and wishes to honour them.)

Hibberd was, by inclination, a turf rather than a seed man. But there were dangers: 'Good turf is a rarity and it is worth any amount of effort of trouble to secure it.' Meadow turf, as recommended by Cobbett and others, was regrettably 'utterly unfit for any garden . . . You must go instead to Mr Lawson of Piccadilly, Mr Clarke of Bishopsgate, Suttons of Reading.' (Hibberd later abandoned this advice, praising the capacity of meadow turf – given time and care – to acquire a texture 'fit for a princess in a fairy tale'.) Worst of all was to sow with the sweepings of haylofts, which 'promises well at first . . .

135

but the first drought burns it brown and the rains that follow bring up thousands of weeds'.

Hibberd's affection for the lawn embraced the feel of it as well as the look. He abhorred grass which was 'like flint to the foot'. While disapproving of plantains, daisies and dandelions, he opened his arms to another invader: 'In my opinion, spite of the dictum of gardeners, a moderate growth of moss is absolutely essential to the thorough beauty and enjoyment of a lawn.' Moss was 'as deliciously soft as a down bed, so that if you would roll about in it in ecstasies at the glory of summer, you are in no danger of bruising your elbows and scapulae'.

To furnish the surface for these scenes of abandon, Hibberd recommended a selection of suitable varieties of seed, including crested dog's tail (*Cynosurus cristatus*), fine-leaved fescue (*Festuca tenuifolia*) and perennial white clover (*Trifolium repens perenne*). As these were also approved by Mrs Loudon, it can be assumed that by the mid-1850s the best nurseries were able to provide the essential commodity whose lack had ever been the lawnsman's chief bugbear; although the reliability of identification and germination continued to be nagging problems.

For Shirley Hibberd, writing in the 1850s, there was already only one sensible way to impose control on cultivated grass: 'A mowing machine keeps a lawn in much better trim than a scythe. The grass can be cut by anyone who has sufficient strength to work an ordinary garden roller; it is therefore particularly well-suited to amateurs who are not used to the scythe.' Although, at a later date, Hibberd found himself undecided between the 'cut-and-scatter' Archimedean and the 'cut-and-collect' Shanks, of the necessity of using a machine to cut grass, he had no doubt.

Like others, he had been entranced, briefly, by the dream of a lawn which had all the aesthetic and moral qualities of grass, but was liberated from the tedious task of eternal mowing. In *The Town Garden*, he was aroused to a passion of enthusiasm by a new species of lawn displayed in the gardens of A. Mongredieu Esq. in Forest Hill –

> a dwarf-growing and tufted alpine plant which forms an unbroken surface of the richest green, heightened in beauty during July by the production of myriads of snow-white blossoms . . . unaffected by drought or frost . . . softer to the foot than a Turkey carpet . . . it never requires mowing . . . the older it gets, the more perfect in its beauty.

But alas, the charms of *Spergula pilifera* – otherwise known as spurry – were a snare and a delusion. And alas for Mssrs Henderson and Sons, nurserymen of St John's Wood, who must have imagined themselves on to a winner when they introduced it. Prolonged acquaintance with its habits revealed incurable character flaws to Hibberd. It could not, after all, tolerate drought, and demanded such labour to be kept free of weeds as to make the old chore of scything seem almost painless. In *The Amateur's Flower Garden*, he recorded wistfully that in the previous two decades he had seen no more than three *Spergula* lawns that were of 'agreeable remembrance'; and he concluded that the troublesome nature of the plant had banished the prospect of the lawn that never needed to be mown.

*

Another promoter of the lawn's virtues was Edward Kemp, chief instrument in the creation of the country's first major municipal park, Birkenhead Park (although it was actually designed by Paxton), and later its salaried superintendent. In 1850 Kemp published his *How to Lay Out a Small Garden,* a dreary and pedagogic attempt to combat what he called 'the incongruity and dullness observable in the majority of gardens'. Whether he diminished or enhanced that dullness is a matter of argument. Unlike Hibberd, he had nothing of great interest to say about lawns, contenting himself with observing that they were cheaper to maintain than flower borders and 'should therefore abound where economy of keeping is sought'; and advising against placing walks and flower beds that destroyed 'the smoothness, continuance and extent of the lawn', and in favour of removing irregularities 'that are quite incompatible with high polish'.

Kemp's books sold in very large numbers, and his dutiful endorsement of the place of the lawn may well have helped persuade the new suburbanites to fall into line. The professional gardener and journalist, Robert Fish, knew a great deal more about grass culture than Kemp, and returned to the subject repeatedly in the column which he wrote for a number of years in the *Gardener's Magazine.* Fish's approach was practical rather than theoretical. He recorded struggles with plantains and daisies, leaves and worms, downpours and droughts. He favoured the mower for efficiency, but retained a soft spot for the scythe, as it kept the lawn 'nice at bottom'. A recurrent theme in Fish's writing was that the supposed economy of the lawn was a myth. A lawn, he wrote towards the end of his life, 'is the most expensive thing in a gentleman's garden'.

But people didn't mind. They may well, in the first place, have laid down their grass because they had been told it was the proper and economical thing to do. But then they found that they liked the lawn for reasons that had little or nothing to do with thrift or the advertised ease of upkeep. They liked it because of the look of it, and the way it helped to fill the garden, and showed off the flowers and shrubs to best advantage. The lawn gave them pride in their homes; and they found that, far from begrudging the expenditure of time, cash and labour that it demanded, they liked it the more for the demands it made.

Thus did the lawn annexe the pleasure grounds of the professional classes. And as it did so, it claimed a place in the public consciousness. Its green blades spread from the pages of the specialized periodicals and books into popular fiction.

The opening scene in Trollope's *The Small House at Allington* takes place upon the lawn outside the Small House, where the obstinately virtuous Lily Dale – the novelist's favourite heroine though not mine – her sister Bel, the Squire's son Bernard and Bernard's shady friend Adolphus Crosbie, destined to be Lily Dale's ruin, stroll forth for croquet and genteel gossip. 'The glory of the Small House', relates Trollope, 'certainly consists in its lawn, which is as smooth, as level, and as much like velvet as grass has ever been made to look.' To Lily Dale, her lawn is a matter of much quiet pride, superior in its absence of tufts to the much broader expanse of turf beside the Great House. The Squire, however, cares nothing for tufts, nor for croquet. His pride has another source: 'He would stand in the middle of the grass plot, surveying his grounds and taking stock of the shrubs and the flowers and the fruit trees around him; for he never forgot that it was all his own.'

Michael Waters, in his study *The Garden In Victorian Literature,* identified the particular usefulness of the lawn on the novelistic stage, in encouraging through its informality private exchanges which were simultaneously open to the narrator's eye. In the first chapter of *The Portrait of a Lady,* Henry James sees the 'wide carpet of turf' outside the country house as 'seeming but the extension of a luxurious interior'. Upon the 'smooth, dense turf' his cast of aristocrats and assorted well-bred idlers sip tea and nibble at sandwiches, while he eavesdrops on the cadences of their refined chat. But neither James nor Trollope displays any curiosity as to how their perfect lawns achieved their perfection. Their interest is restricted to exploiting them as a setting for the manipulation of characters.

For a fuller appreciation of the dramatic possibilities of grass and its cultivation, we must turn to one in the very long string of now forgotten romances by the once immensely popular Rhoda Broughton. In her novel of 1886, *Doctor Cupid,* this clergyman's daughter presented a scene of such wondrous absurdity and throbbing, half-suppressed sexuality as to make any subsequent lawn-based encounter short of a satanic orgy necessarily tame. Since no one, apart from the most assiduous student of third-rate Victorian fiction is likely to have heard of the book, let alone to have read it, it is worth looking at in a little detail.

The situation is thus: the hero, John Talbot, is supposed to be in love with malicious, married Lady Betty Harborough, the failings of whose character are suggested by her fondness for lounging in a hammock, smoking cigarettes and reading the Sunday papers; but in fact his heart belongs to sweet Betty. She has a lawn in need of mowing, and has been lent a machine by 'milady' to do it; but her man, Jacob, has fallen ill and the boy who would normally help him is 'out vagranting'. John Talbot's eyes are 'bent upon the sward, today not shorn to quite its normal pitch of velvet nicety'. He is moved to an outrageous suggestion:

> 'Why should I not mow?' asks he at last.
>   'You?'
>   'Yes, I; and you lead the pony.'
>   'Is that a joke?'
>   'A joke – no! Will you tell me where the pony is? May I harness it?'

Betty looks at him, and the grass, already an inch and a half long, and yields. They harness the pony, place the animal's feet in its mowing shoes.

> They set off. Loudly whirrs the machine. Up flies the grass in a little green cloud, which the sun instantly turns to deliciously-scented new-mown hay.

The noise precludes much in the way of conversation. But that does not trouble John Talbot, marching behind his beloved, as he feasts his eyes on her 'flat back, her noble shoulders, the milky nape of her neck'. As for Betty:

> Her eye, flattered by her shaven lawn, cannot rest
> very severely upon him who has shaven it for her.
> Her spirits have risen; exhilarated by the wholesome
> exercise, by the sunshine, by who knows what?

Who indeed? Could it be that Betty of the flat back and noble shoulders is a-tremble at the thought of her fellow mower, unclothed in the warm, soft herbage, hands greened with grass stains reaching out for her ardent flesh? I think so.

Tempting though it is to speculate on the basis of this scorching stuff that the Victorian enthusiasm for the lawn may have had some deep sexual taproot, the truth is probably more prosaic. Certainly, the *Gardener's Chronicle* seems to have been unaware of any latent erotic element. 'The ornamental grass plot in front of the mansion or cottage is to gardening what the stockpot is to cooking,' it stated in 1874. The lawn's ascendancy was hardly challenged, but other aspects of Victorian gardening were, and remain, more contentious. The enthusiasm for imported species of conifer and the deployment of coloured gravel, the mania for glass-houses (Paxton's 'Hot-houses for the Million' were launched in the early 1850s) and for filling borders with contrasting blocks of massed perlargoniums, lobelias, petunias and the like, aroused controversy at the time, and have been viewed with something akin to a shudder by subsequent authorities. Robin Lane Fox wrote in extreme terms: 'Grand Victorian gardens are ghastly . . . insensitive and flashy . . . imperious assertion and mere show . . . precision and swiftly-attained exactness . . . made by men in a hurry.'

Lane Fox's hero, champion in the defence of traditional English values against garish foreign invaders and the worship of ever more ingenious mechanical wonders, was William Robinson. In books such as *The English Flower Garden* and *The Wild Garden*, Robinson trumpeted the virtues of the cottage garden tradition and of hardy, self-reliant climbers and shrubs, and railed against the 'pastry-book gardening' represented by bedding out. His particular *bête noire* was an extravagance regarded by conventional opinion of the time as one of the wonders of the world, the Crystal Palace at Sydenham; where Paxton had created around his glass cathedral a Victorian version of Versailles, a geometric masterplan of cascades, fountains, arcades and terraces organized by a mighty central axis into rigid symmetry. It was an overwhelming statement of Man's mastery over, and divorce from, Nature. Robinson's alternative 'natural style' – in truth, rather imprecisely articulated – embraced beds filled with roses, shrubs and hardy plants, flowering creepers tangled over walls, and wide lawns. But devotion to manicured turf irritated him:

> Mowing the grass once a fortnight in pleasure grounds, as now commonly practised, is a costly mistake. We want shaven carpets of grass here and there, but what nonsense it is for them to be shaved as often as foolish men shave their faces! Think of the labour involved in the ridiculous work of cutting the heads off flowers and grass.

William Robinson's objections were not widely shared. The pride taken by the late Victorians in the regular care of their lawns acquired a nationalistic tinge reminiscent of Pepys's comment about the inferiority of Continentals in the matter. A fanciful snapshot much favoured by gardening journalists was of the foreigner, humbled by the splendour of the English garden in its glory, goggle-eyed with amazement at the perfection of its sward. The French gardening authority, Edouard André, conceded the case: 'The most beautiful lawns are found in England,' he wrote in 1879. 'Under the influence of a foggy climate, fertile soil, repeated mowings and rigorous weeding, you obtain these short lawns, as fine as moss, both soft and firm, as even as a carpet.'

The mower industry responded energetically and profitably to the challenge of assisting in this pursuit of British excellence. New models continued to pour on to the market, accompanied by new gadgets: lawn sprinklers, mechanical grass and leaf collectors and the like. Some of the new mowers came from America: the 'latest improved Junior Archimedean' with cutters extended to match the width of the side wheels; the 'Great American BALL BEARING Lawn Mower (the easiest-running machine made)' from the Supplee Hardware Co. in Philadelphia; the Columbia from Richmond, Indiana ('for perfect work and general satisfaction no Dealer or Jobber can afford to overlook it'). Lesser-known British firms strived for resonance in their branding: the Invincible from Crowley and Co; the Balmoral from Hartley and Sugden; the Imperial from Picksley, Sims and Co; the Excelsior from Waite, Burnell and Huggins. Others sought to conjure associations of lightness and convenience: Hirst and Co. with the Charm; Holt and Willis with the Easy; F. Lasseter (an Australian firm) with the Fairy.

The drawback with all the larger machines, in spite of great advances in efficiency and smoothness, was the muscle-power required to operate them. The first step towards a power-driven mower was obvious: steam. In 1893 James Sumner, a Lancashire blacksmith, patented a steam-powered mower, using the engine from a motorized tricycle he had devised. It was fired by petroleum or paraffin, and after various adaptations was manufactured by the Leyland Steam Motor Company, which was eventually to metamorphose into British Leyland.

In 1897 two models were offered for sale – a 25-inch machine at £60, and one of 30 inches at £90. Green and Shanks followed the same route, both companies marketing steam-powered mowers at or soon after the turn of the century. But their considerable cost, great size, massive weight (around one and a half tons) and unwieldiness combined to make them little more than impressive curiosities, whose clankings and puffings and enormous turning circles were confined to a few sports grounds and country estates. Their time never came, for the flair and imagination of one of those Ipswich Ransomes made them redundant before they were properly born.

In 1899, according to the Ransomes archive, James Ransome was working on the development of a petrol-driven mower. He did not invent it, but he seized upon its potential. Three years later, the company introduced the first model. Forty-two inches wide, powered by a six-horsepower engine, and weighing several hundred-weight, it was a juggernaut, a gleaming, roaring beast of a machine; but delicate and amenable compared with its steam-powered rival. Edward VII had the two matched on the lawns at Buckingham Palace, and declared the Ransomes the winner. Cricket's bearded colossus, W. G.

145

Grace, ordered one for his London County Cricket Club at Crystal Palace, and declared that every self-respecting club should do the same, as 'whenever the ground is soft you could get on it with a motor mower when it would be impossible for a horse machine to be used without harm to the ground'. Mr Prestcott Westcar of Herne Bay bought the first, Cadbury Brothers the second, for their sports ground at Bournville; and the steam mower was doomed to the museum.

Although it would be many years before the pony and horse-drawn mowers followed the path of the steam machine, it is convenient to see an age ending with the introduction of James Ransome's brainchild. The year before, the Queen whose reign had begun when Edwin Budding's mind was still buzzing, had died. During that span of time much had happened: an empire had been extended, a society transformed, the appearance of the country changed beyond recognition. And a passion had been born and come of age, consummated for hosts of ordinary people in the private, personal space around their homes, which they called their gardens. A part of that space was green grass. It had stamped itself on the new suburban geography. At the same time, it had acquired a metaphysical dimension, contributing in a particular way to that collective sense of Englishness or Britishness which seems to us such a powerful character-istic of the age; one now lost, and never likely to be recaptured. The lawn was an aspect of British particu-larity. Its colour, its texture, its associations, the rituals attending its nurture, were an expression of Britishness. A generation later, this sentiment, suffused with an inten-sity of nostalgia derived from violent schism with the past, was expressed by the gardening historian, Eleanor Sinclair Rohde:

> The green lawns of this country are still the admiration of the world. The beauty of the matchless lawns in college quadrangles remains for ever in the memory, and lawns are still the chief beauty of many of our most famous gardens. The methods of making them and maintaining them lack the picturesqueness of olden days, though there are still gardens where the discordant sound of the lawn mower is never heard, and the lawns are shorn by men come from generations skilled in the art of the scythe . . . The foreigner admires, but even with all the resources of science, cannot hope to make lawns to compare with the deep velvety texture of our lawns . . . For those of us who live in the Old Country, and those of us whose lot is cast in the great dominions beyond the seas, are equally proud of the fact that in the 'islands of the West' we have the greenest and the most beautiful grass in the world.

Velvet Robes

Lawns are nature purged of death and sex. No wonder Americans like them so much

MICHAEL POLLAN

I t is curious that two of the first three American presidents should have contributed significantly towards the development of the American lawn, whereas I have come across no evidence of any British head of state or government evincing anything more than the most superficial interest in grass cultivation. I suppose it has something to do with this: that while in Britain, the lawn evolved over centuries in an episodic and haphazard fashion dictated by the slow maturing of popular taste, in the United States it was, almost from the first, accompanied by and directed by a notion of civic responsibility. The Americans took our randomly assembled ornamental grass culture, adapted it to their own circumstances, and superimposed upon it moral connotations which were to result, within a few generations, in the fairly general acceptance of the axiom that a man's worth to society was reflected in, and could to a considerable degree be judged by, the condition of his lawn.

*

At Mount Vernon, beyond the Potomac, George Washington ordered a bowling green and a deer park, the two separated physically if not visibly by a ha-ha, in the English fashion. An entry in Washington's diary for 1785 identifies him as the first American lawn champion:

> The appearance of the day and the impracticability of giving, on account of the clamminess of the day, an even face to any more of my lawn until the ground should get dryer, of which there is no immediate prospect, I sowed what was levelled and smoothed of it with English grass seeds; and as soon as the top was so dry as not to stick to the roller, I rolled and cross-rolled it.

Prints displaying the glories of the first president's home became extremely popular, and stimulated the imitation by a few wealthy Americans of the English model of mansion surrounded by parkland. A Mrs Pinckney, recently returned from her European tour, had a lawn laid down by her home in South Carolina. Mr William Hamilton commissioned one in Philadelphia, and General Hartwell Cocke complemented his Palladian pile in Fluranna County, Virginia, with an appropriate expanse of trimmed turf. But the idea that smooth, cultivated grass might act as a vegetable stimulant to the virtues of responsibility and citizenship belonged to Thomas Jefferson. The home he built at Monticello in Virginia was intended as an American reinvention of the cultural influences which had so enthused him during his years in Europe. Jefferson's concept – of a vista flowing from the mansion through the lawned garden fringed by trees to the foothills of the Blue Ridge Mountains – was designed as an expression of national aspiration. Under his direction, it became the University of Virginia, known to generations of its graduates as, simply, The Lawn.

In spite of Jefferson's example, Americans in general had more pressing matters on their minds than the benefits of cultivated grass. The native grasses encountered by the first settlers had been annuals. The livestock ate them, and then mostly died – either because they were poisonous, or because it would not grow again. As early as the 1630s, new arrivals were being exhorted to bring grass and clover seed with them, to provide pasturage. That utilitarian example persisted. Seed was sown so that the stomach might be filled, not to delight the eye. Making a new country permitted little time and energy for the refinements of horticulture. Visitors from Europe, such as Cobbett and Dickens, were struck by the untidiness that attended the rapid maturing of a nation. 'The well-trimmed lawns and green meadows of home are not here,' observed Dickens, somewhat truistically. 'And the grass, compared with our ornamental plots and pastures, is rank and wild.'

The birth of the American suburban ideal, of a detached house standing in its plot, occurred, roughly speaking, in the second half of the 19th century. According to Kenneth T. Jackson's brilliant study, *The Crabgrass Frontier*, the spiritual need for space and the corresponding aspiration to live away from the city arose in the first instance from the fear of epidemic diseases such as cholera and yellow fever; and was encouraged by liberation from what had been an acute, constant and largely justifiable fear of nature. As communities were established and grew, those who lived in them felt more secure. Distanced and protected from the perils of the wilderness, they began to see the outdoors as noble and benign in character, rather than dangerous. The space around the new suburban residence became an opportunity for the beneficial virtues of nature, suitably tamed and civilized, to be constantly enjoyed.

At the same time, a crucial divergence from the English suburban model emerged. The Englishman's garden was a private matter for himself. Shielded from passing eyes by his house, enclosed in walls, fences and hedges, obscured by tree and shrubs, it was a place of his own. To be sure, he often needed advice on what to do with it; and in the absence of useful ideas of his own, he was liable to subscribe to monotonous uniformity. But whether he did or not was his business, because the world at large was kept at bay. He could indulge his individuality, pursue his own taste for the exotic or the barbarous, in privacy; indeed, in seclusion and even secrecy. But the Americans, moved by a powerful common trust in, and dependence on, the community and its attendant ideals of citizenship, went the other way. They declined to build walls and grow hedges, and hide their homes behind barriers of vegetation. And having established their own way, they set about bolstering it with a moral legitimacy. From the start, the lawn was invested with a righteousness which it has yet to forfeit.

The first acknowledged authority on American garden design was Andrew Jackson Downing, who – had he not perished at the age of thirty-seven in a fire on a Hudson River steamer, displaying, according to the contemporary accounts, an almost inhuman degree of cool courage – would surely have become the prime shaper of the suburban ideal. As it was, his practical work was mostly done on behalf of a select handful of plutocrats in the eastern states. But his writing reached a wide audience. In one of his 'Rural Essays', Downing identifies grass, water and trees as the trinity of essential elements. His apprehension of grass is sensual – 'the soft turf . . . thrown like a smooth natural carpet over the swelling outline of the trembling earth . . . a perfect wonder of tufted freshness and verdure'. Downing proceeds to offer practical advice: the deployment of two yoke of oxen to plough the ground, thorough trenching, the removal of every stone, the sowing at two bushels to the acre of mixed *Agrostis vulgaris* and *Trifolium repens,* and the use in mowing of 'an English scythe' of the most perfect temper and quality, with an edge like a razor. He returns to the sermon: 'No expenditure in ornamental garden-ing is productive of so much beauty as that incurred in producing a well-kept lawn. It is a universal passport to admiration.'

Downing died in 1852. In the same year, Alexander Jackson Davis was chosen to design what was to be the world's first 'picturesque suburb', Llewellyn Park, in the Orange Mountains to the west of Manhattan. Downing's precepts – among them that 'the close proximity of fences to a house gives the whole place a confined and mean character' – were a powerful influence on Davis's Utopian concept. His declared principle was to be guided by nature's bequest. Much of the woodland and underbrush was retained, to give the place an unthreat-eningly sylvan air. Winding lanes followed the contours of the land, and the principal route through the 50,000 acres was curvilinear. Civilization's more sordid manifestations – shops, factories, the slaughterhouse – were banished. The average size of each plot was three acres, and a committee of management was elected to ensure that these were maintained in a manner in keeping with the ethos. Llewellyn Park was intended as a model for a new mode of communal existence, proclaimed by its architects to be progressive and democratic. In fact, from the start it was exclusive and discriminatory, suburban bliss made available by invitation to those with the approved attitudes, the required contacts and the wealth.

Llewellyn Park established the direction of a movement which was brought to fulfilment in the suburban designs of Frederick Law Olmsted and Calvert Vaux, and codified in the writings of Frank Jessup Scott. Among the suburbs laid out by Olmsted before he devoted himself to New York's Central Park, the most celebrated was Riverside, on the edge of Chicago. Olmsted intended the suburb to be, not a refuge from the obnoxious city, but an integration between the best of city and country. Its purpose was to refresh the spirit of the city worker when he returned from his labours, and it therefore had to be pleasing in a convenient, well-ordered way. There must be parks, lakes, commons – places where nature's healing influences were readily available. The roads must be curved, the spacious homes set back thirty feet 'to suggest and imply leisure, contemplativeness and happy tranquillity'.

But the pleasures were accompanied by duties. The man admitted to communion with these blessings was expected to give something back. For the suburb to function properly, to give of its best, the residents must subscribe to the suburban code. It was their charge and their

pleasure to keep their houses tidy, and their gardens –
the paradisal borders to the shaded lanes – in an unblem-
ished condition. The moral force of the obligation to
conform was irresistible, and it easily bred intolerance.
The chief propagandist on behalf of the suburban paradise was Frank Jessup Scott, and it was he who laid down
the regulation dealing with the front garden, or front
yard: 'It is unchristian to hedge from the sight of others
the beauties of Nature which it has been our good fortune to create ... Throwing front grounds together
enriches all who take part in the exchange.' 'Let your
lawn be your home's velvet robe,' he wrote, 'and your
flowers its not too promiscuous decoration.'

Scott's *The Art of Beautifying Suburban Home Grounds* is
the most complete expression of the philosophy which
inspired the creators of the first suburbs. The principal
drawback of the English aristocratic model – the stately
home in its park – is characterized by Scott as 'the isolation and loneliness of the habitual inmates of the house
– the ladies'. No one can be happy thus, he contends;
we were not meant to live in this way.

> Our panacea is to take country life as a famishing
> man should take food ... in very small quantities.
> From half an acre to four or five acres will afford
> ground enough to give all the finer pleasures of
> country life. This kind of half-country, half-town life
> is the happy medium and the realizable ideal for the
> majority of well-to-do Americans.

When it came to realizing the ideal, there was only
one starting point:

> Of all the external decorations of a home, a well-kept
> lawn is the most essential. Preserve in one or two

154

places the greatest length of unbroken lawn that the space will admit of . . . a smooth closely-shaven surface of grass . . . Neatness and order are as essential to the pleasing effect of ground furniture as of house furniture. No matter how elegant or appropriate the latter may be, it will never look well in the home of a slattern.

To avoid any such imputation, the lawn had to be cut at least once a week. Fortunately – technological progress coming to the aid of moral imperative – 'the admirable little hand-mowing machines' had arrived upon the scene. The vision of suburbanites who 'may have the pleasure of doing their own mowing without the wearisome bending of the back incident to the use of the scythe' moved Scott to a state of spiritual ecstasy:

Whoever spends the early hours of one summer day, while the dew spangles the grass, in pushing these grass cutters over a velvety lawn, breathing the fresh sweetness of the morning and the perfume of new-mown hay, will never rest contented again in the city.

The link between the condition of a lawn and the moral rectitude or otherwise of its owner was established overtly and explicitly in the United States, whereas in Britain it has remained, if it can be said to have taken root at all, nebulous and implicit. This may well explain why, in America, the science of grass culture secured governmental backing and financial support at an early stage, while in Britain it has never enjoyed these dubious blessings. The lawn became a facet of the 'American way of life', one to which it was deemed proper to devote scientific and economic resources. If grass was intrinsically good, it followed that better grass must be better. A powerful research impetus took hold, and with it the notion of achievable perfection.

The way towards that goal was opened by the mechanical mower. The first patents for American lawn-mowers were registered in 1868, and the possibilities they offered were embraced with enthusiasm. For a time the choice of what sort of lawn to grow escaped the attention of the arbiters of propriety. In a book published in 1888, Charles Flint recommended a mixture of meadow foxtail, various fescues, ryegrass of two or three types, timothy, conventional meadow grass and assorted clover: a diversity capable of producing a pleasing lawn without excessive labour in a wide variety of soil and climatic conditions. But the puritan tendency was already at work.

By the late 1890s standards of correctness in lawn care were being laid down by the new United States Department of Agriculture. The chief authority was the senior agronomist, F. Lamson-Scribner. His primary article of faith was hardly original – that 'nothing is more beautiful than a well-kept lawn ... the most fascinating and delightful feature in landscape gardening'. But this banality was then invested with a moral dimension bordering on the sinister: 'There is nothing which more strongly bespeaks the character of the owner than the treatment and adornment of lawns upon his place.'

Secure on his high plateau of virtue, Lamson-Scribner looked out over his land of opportunity – encompassing sun-blasted plain, forested hills, tropical swamps and temperate, rolling farmland, with every variety of climatic condition known on earth – and arrogated to himself the task of deciding what constituted the proper American lawn. There could be no bastardizing of seed. The sole true way was 'a single variety of grass, with a smooth even surface, uniform colour, and an elastic turf which has become, through constant care, so fine and so close in texture as to exclude weeds which, when appearing, should at once be removed'.

In 1901 the American Congress voted a budget of $17,000 for the study of grass cultivation. It was a declaration of intent and independence. America acknowledged that the little island across the Atlantic, uniquely favoured for the purpose by its climate and history, had given birth to the lawn and had led the way in the first stages of social and mechanical development. But that chapter was closed. From now on, America was to take the lead. America, building on the accidental achievement and commendable but limited curiosity of the British, would show what could be done. Human ingenuity, nourished by energy, cash and a sense of civic pride and responsibility, would achieve perfection; which, in the American way, would then be made available to all who could afford it. Forget nature, forget diversity, forget that the people were spread across desert, swamp and mountain, in conditions as different from the gentle climes of the north-east as from those on the surface of the moon. A myth was made, the Holy Grail of the Promised Lawn offered in a plot of one-third of an acre outside the front door.

This vision has driven the evolution of the American lawn in the 20th century. It was, of course, a fraud, a snare and a delusion. But it was so cunningly packaged, its appearance so temptingly accessible: a mere expanse of vegetation. The means to achieve it were readily available: seed, machinery, tonics to promote health, weapons against enemies. All that was required, it seemed, was effort and careful attention to the words of the high priests. And when the vision proved elusive, the reasons were at hand. The seed was not right. The machine was defective. The range of aids was too primitive, the enemies too numerous and resourceful, the expert words not expert enough, the effort and commitment insufficient.

We may acquit that obscure agronomist, Lamson-Scribner, of motives of materialism. He doubtless believed that he had identified a moral truth, and in doing so had advanced the cause of progress. He was not to know that behind him would come men of capitalist inclination, intent on exploiting his preaching, not for the benefit of mankind, but to do business. They would apprehend that the vision of the Promised Lawn could never be achieved; but that considerable commercial possibilities might be realized by concealing this fact from those inspired by the ideal. The search for the Grail spurred a flood of words, a clanking armoury of hardware, an arsenal of chemical weapons, an incalculable expenditure of time, effort and cash. And still it remains where Grails were meant to be: just out of reach.

F. Scott Fitzgerald exploited the convention that a man could be judged by the size and condition of his lawn to telling effect in *The Great Gatsby*. From Gatsby's mansion on Long Island stretch great sweeps of resplendent turf, down to the sea and across to the boundary with the property of his neighbour, Nick Carraway – the narrator of the story, a man whose lack of social consequence is reflected in his paltry, scruffy grass. Carraway is neither surprised nor affronted when Gatsby's gardener arrives with mower to 'erase the dark line where my ragged lawn ended and the darker, well-kempt expanse of his began'. There is no physical barrier between the two, but economically and socially that dark line is a chasm between one who matters and one who does not. One of the morals of the tale is the fragility and impermanence of status. At the end, when Gatsby is dead and his greatness has been brought to nothing, Nick find that 'the grass in his lawn had grown as long as mine'.

A burgeoning turf industry fastened upon the convention. A promotion on behalf of the Coldwell Lawn Mower proclaimed the message: 'The observer invariably judges the character of a homeowner by the care that is given to the lawn. Seldom, if ever, do you find the owner of a magnificent home neglecting his lawn.'

A Coldwell mower would doubtless assist in the acquisition of status. But the question was: were its cutters engaging with the right stuff?

The pull of the English ideal was still powerful. Barwell's Imported English Seed Mixture promised the discerning purchaser the chance to

> possess the perfect English lawn. Old England's historic estates are carpeted with the most beautiful stretches of lawn. Through centuries of careful study and trial, coarse undesirable grasses have been supplanted by a uniform durable species, almost the texture of velvet . . .

This nonsense dates from 1911. A few years later, in 1917, an alliance was formed which was to dictate the direction of turf research to the present day. Its focus was on providing an American solution to an American need, and the first requirements were cash and power. Both became available in abundance when the United States Department of Agriculture joined forces with the United States Golf Association.

Golf is a game, or – according to Arthur Ransome – 'a laborious form of open-air patience in which you hit a ball, walk earnestly after it, and hit it again'. But in the United States, within a matter of decades after the laying of the first course at Ardsley, New York, in 1888, it became a powerful social force. It combined many characteristics which could double as social aspirations. It was healthy, but not arduous; competitive, but not dangerously so; outdoors, but not of the wilderness; solitary and sociable. It could be enjoyed by the young, those in the prime of life, and the ancient; by men and women; by the exceedingly rich, the aspiring rich, and the merely well-to-do (though generally in different places). It could be played for fun, or for money; by amateurs and professionals, by bunglers and geniuses. It reflected society, and society's organizing structures transferred very easily to the golf club. Golf had to be codified. There must be committees to draw up the rules, arrange the matches, appoint the officers, issue decrees on dress, manners, who was to be allowed into what bar at what time, with whom. It had the comforting air of being democratic, while in fact being organized hierarchically, those with the most money and the best contacts being found at the top. Its allure was felt by all sections of the white, professional classes, as well as by the idle rich. In time, the embrace between the golf club and society would become closer still, with the evolution of the 'fairway lifestyle', whose physical manifestation was a golf course into which the homes of the members were integrated.

The rich men who formed the golf clubs required the best of everything – starting with the best possible surface on which to strike their white balls. And they were prepared to pay for it. In 1916 a seed company, O. M. Scott and Sons, from Marysville, Ohio, supplied five thousand pounds of bluegrass seed to the Brentwood Golf Club on Long Island. It did not take Scott and Sons long to awaken to the potential of this market; and not much longer after that to start exploring the even greater possibilities of representing the standards of the putting green as suitable for the domestic lawn. In 1928 the partnership between the Department of Agriculture and the US Golf Association was cemented by the setting up of a research station at Arlington where a swarm of experts were to be found poring over five hundred experimental plots of grass. The seedsmen from Ohio were in the vanguard of the movement which sought to persuade the American consumer that the fruits of this boffinry were available to him. 'Scotts' Creeping Bent for Perfect Lawns! Sod in six weeks! A rich velvety stretch of lawn that chokes weeds before they can grow! A deep, thick uniform turf that makes your home a beauty spot . . . like the deep green pile of a Turkish carpet . . .'

The alliance of government and golf had by now become tripartite, with the recruitment of the Gardening Club of America. The Gardening Club's newsletter was the ideal means to spread the word of Mr Lamson-Scribner as made real in the rich earth of the Arlington research station. The glad tidings that the Promised Lawn was at hand went forth to millions of aspiring households.

But all the exhortations and soothing scientific counsel could not disguise an awkward truth. For a combination of climatic, economic and sociological reasons, none of these super-refined single species of grass seed was remotely suitable for the domestic lawn. There was a deep divide between the putting green with its support system of green-keepers armed with every machine and chemical science could devise, and the front or back yard stretch of turf dependent on its untutored owner, with a living to earn and a budget to manage. The proportions of that divide were implicitly recognized in a Garden Club newsletter of 1931 which advised that the lawn needed to be completely remade *each spring and autumn*.

The Wall Street Crash, the depression and the Second World War put a brake on the spread of the American lawn. But its place in that complex system of symbols known as the American Way was already secure. In 1944 the magazine *House Beautiful* enlisted its appeal in the war effort: 'Wherever the GI is he dreams of velvety lawns, beautiful flowers ... he wants to come home to them. Keep them growing their best, awaiting that day! They will contribute immeasurably toward a winning home front.'

The end of the conflict and the return of the GIs to the land of promise initiated the biggest sustained house-building boom in history. 'How can we expect to sell democracy in Europe until we prove that within the democratic system we can provide decent homes for our people?' demanded Harry Truman during his 1948 presidential campaign. Once elected, he and Congress engineered the release of tens of billions of dollars to elevate a generation into a new home-owning middle class. Each year between 1947 and 1964, an average of one and a quarter million new homes came into being, almost all of them on plots which society dictated were, or should become, lawns. It is estimated that in 1960 there were thirty million American lawns, a total which was being added to at the rate of at least half a million each year.

The ideological orthodoxy, linking a man's lawn with his worth, remained unchallenged, and indeed strengthened its hold. People moving into what was to become the single most celebrated new housing development in America – Levittown, on Long Island, a cityless suburb of seventeen thousand box-like homes – were required by the creator, William Levitt, to sign a contract obliging them to 'cut or cause to be cut the lawn at least once a week between April 1st and November 15th'. If they failed, the grass was cut for them and they were charged.

'Not to mow', stated the magazine *Better Homes and Gardens*, 'is to attack one's neighbours, lowering the value of their homes and calling into question the integrity of the street and the cultural norms it represents.' What had begun as a convention rapidly acquired the force almost of statute, its moral logic demanding wider application. In 1950 the vice-president of the mighty corporation which had blossomed from that Ohio seed company, Charles B. Mills of Scotts, asserted that the condition of municipal lawns mirrored government probity as surely as that of home lawns reflected family virtue. The lesson according to Scotts went out across the land, via the company's long-established newsletter, which by 1960 had four million subscribers.

The task of educating the multitudes of new homeowners inspired the turfgrass industry to prodigies of technical and marketing effort, and to a massively profitable expansion. In his homily on the moral importance of the lawn, Mr Mills listed the equipment required to keep its virtue in top condition. The hardware comprised mower, aerator, perforator, cart, sprinkler, sweeper and roller; all to be supported by a complex system of nutrients and poisons. The arming of the American homeowner for his yard crusade mushroomed into a multi-billion dollar industry.

The attendant marketing propaganda was overwhelmingly masculine in tone and direction, even when – as in this 1953 promotion – a nod was attempted to the female of the species:

> Mowing is a man's job ... but here's a tip for wives whose husbands are about to buy a mower. Unless your lawn is the kind that obligingly stops growing when hubby just can't find time to mow it, you'd better slip your arm through his when he goes mower shopping ... make sure it's one you can handle.

In general, though, the message was insistently male-oriented: 'Which house's boss has the Clemson? The one with the well-trimmed lawn, every time.'

Nor could women reasonably be expected to involve themselves in the chemical side of the campaign. It required a soldier's mind to comprehend the variety of adversaries ranged against the lawn, and to understand how the corresponding array of counter-measures should be deployed.

The lawn's foes were grouped into two categories: vegetable and animal. Among the factions in the vegetable camp were plantains, dandelions, ragweed and the like. But the worst was crabgrass. At its most innocent, it would make your lawn 'look as unkempt as a man with a three-day beard'. More often, it was likened to a fifth columnist, malignantly dedicated to the sabotage and overthrow of an American institution. In the early days, the recommended treatments were based on either arsenate or mercury, both of which were toxic to humans and animals, and neither of which was very effective. Then came cyanamide, and then potassium cyanate, with the command: 'Knock out your lawn's worst enemy . . . KILL IT SO IT STAYS KILLED.'

But it was little use exterminating the weeds if what was left was devoured or destroyed by beasts. Like the enemy in the Malayan jungle, invisible but deadly, the creatures were swarming in to do their evil work: grubs, beetles, caterpillars, cockchafers, earwigs, ants, worms. Once again the scientists came to the rescue, with a chemical dichlorodiphenyltrichloroethane, known affectionately as DDT. 'The atomic bomb of the insect world' they characterized it affectionately. Nothing could stand against it. The creeping, chomping hordes were routed. Used in conjunction with chlordane – which obliterated earthworms and the hated Japanese beetle grub – DDT saved the American lawn from its enemies.

At the same time that the laboratory scientists were devising new methods of destruction, the agronomists at the research stations were grappling with the enduring problem of what grass to grow. The single species doctrine of Lamson-Scribner had proved unsustainable in the face of climatic realities. One early success seemed to realize the dream of Frederick Winslow Taylor of time-and-motion fame, who spent the last years of his life scrutinizing a vast assembly of sods from all over the world, and forecast that one day it would be possible to produce grass 'in much the same way that an article is manufactured in a machine shop or factory'. In 1950 this panacea went on the market, grass seed planted in factory-made sheets of cellulose which was to be cut into the required shape. 'Thousands of home-owners now have a weapon with which to outwit their old enemy, Mother Nature,' the advertisements proclaimed.

For a time in the fifties, a new grass, zoysia, was hailed as the answer to contemporary needs. But gradually, the practice of mixing varieties of seed gained ground. North of Washington DC, the climate smiled upon a blend of fescues, bents, meadow grass and perennial ryegrass. In the southern states, seedsmen would recommend zoysia, bahua, Bermuda grass and centipede grass. Whatever was grown, the essence of the marketing strategy was to intimate that it was not good enough; and simultaneously to hold up, at a tantalizing distance, that remarkably well-preserved phantom, the Promised Lawn. The objective was to persuade the consumer that the acquisition of a new machine, the sowing of a new variety of seed, another application of fertilizer, another contract with that helpful lawn care company, would persuade the phantom to take on flesh.

The strategy was triumphantly successful. The maxim

that 'the grass is greener...' reflected a deep-seated source of inadequacy; a study carried out in Virginia in the early 1980s found that 80 per cent of home-owners believed, and were worried, that their lawns were average or below average. The grip exercised by the orthodoxy became unshakeable. By 1992 four-fifths of the thirty million acres of space around American detached houses was lawn. More than fifty million Americans personally tended lawns (a third more than bothered with flowers, nearly ten times as many as were interested in growing fruit). Seven and half billion dollars was being spent annually on lawn care. (A darker side to this otherwise glowing moon was the steady increase in mowing accidents, to more than sixty thousand in 1989.)

The confirmation in the collective consciousness of the bond between home and lawn, home provider and lawn care, was immune to serious challenge. But it could be gently mocked, as in an article in *Life Magazine* in 1969:

> Let a man drink or default, cheat on his taxes or cheat on his wife, and the community will find forgiveness in its heart. But let him fail to keep his front lawn mown, and be seen doing it, and those hearts will turn to stone. For the American front lawn is a holy place, constantly worshipped but never used. Only its high priest, the American husband, may set foot on it, and then only to perform the sacred rites: mowing with a mower, edging with an edger, sprinkling with a sprinkler, and rooting with a rooter to purify the temple of profane weeds.

By this time Rachel Carson had produced her famous clarion call on behalf of what was to become known as 'the environment', *Silent Spring*, in which she drew her countrymen's attention to the destruction and despoilment being wrought on their world in the name of progress. Concern was focussed on the atrocious effects resulting from the massive use of DDT, which was banned in 1972. It was succeeded by Diazinon, which was gratefully embraced by the turfgrass industry and energetically promoted; until it, too, was indicted for killing wildlife and suspected links with cancer, skin rash, and damage to liver and other organs, and outlawed. Other toxins went the same way, among them parathion (once warmly recommended to gardeners by John C. Shread of the Connecticut Experiment Station, with the caution that it was 'extremely injurious to humans and animals'); and the worm exterminator, chlordane, whose passing is to this day mourned by many lawn care professionals.

Even though the more obviously destructive lawn care aids have now disappeared, the environmental attack on the American lawn has intensified over the past twenty years. A book by Herbert Bormann and other eco-scientists, *Redesigning the American Lawn*, attempted to polarize the arguments around two alternatives. One is what the authors define as the Freedom Lawn, in which a host of different plants – among them dandelions, violets, bluets, spurry, chickweed, timothy and quackgrass – flourish in mutual tolerance, adapting with untidy but comfortable ease to the vagaries of climate, extending an open invitation to any bird, beast, insect or invertebrate which fancies dropping by, in harmony with owner and the world around. The other is the Industrial Lawn, a 'chemically dependent eco-system', weed-free, pest-free, continuously green, relentlessly mown, wholly unattuned to its setting, never wholly achievable, thirsty (average annual requirement ten thousand gallons of water), vastly expensive, vastly lucrative.

While the eco-warriors hammered away at the wastefulness and destructiveness inherent in the lawn faith, others concentrated on its central tenet, its claim to virtue. Chief among these has been the writer Michael Pollan. He analyses the doctrine that the lawn 'looks sort of natural – it's green, it grows'. But he finds appearance and reality at odds: 'In fact it represents a subjugation of the forest as utter and complete as a parking lot.' Pollan's judgement is: 'A lawn is nature under totalitarian rule.'

In a chapter in his book *Second Nature*, Pollan mocks the tyranny of the faith and the way in which society endeavours to enforce conformity (he relates the story of the Thoreau scholar whose wildflower meadow falls foul of a local by-law prohibiting 'noxious weeds'). He wrinkles his nose at 'the unmistakeable odour of virtue that hovers in this country over a scrupulously maintained lawn', and repudiates the tyranny of 'civilization's knife' – the mower. Pollan pushes his rebellion against conformity to the ultimate, by declaring publicly his intention to plant a hedge along his boundary.

The murmur of dissent continues to be heard, but the established religion still prevails. In 1991 Michael Pollan wrote an editorial in the *New York Times* calling on the President to have the lawns surrounding the White House dug up and replaced by wetlands, meadows, vegetable gardens and apple orchards. His cry was not heeded. The seat of government continues to nestle in Frank Jessup Scott's 'velvet robe', seeking to exemplify

– however ludicrously, given the antics of some incumbents – Charles B. Mills's dictum about public and private probity. The mowers hum, sprinklers throw their spray, washing into the emerald turf the prescribed cocktails of fertilizer, herbicide and pesticide.

For who, beyond a handful of vegans, fruitists, Thoreauphiles, wilderness freaks, back-to-nature fanatics and other assorted eco-maniacs, actually wants a Freedom Lawn? Robert W. Schery, former head of the Lawn Institute – the lobbying mouthpiece of the American turfgrass industry – asked and answered the question some years ago: 'Who wants a fare of crabgrass and dandelions, lawn seed swept up from the haymow, non-powered, cast-iron push-mowers, fresh manure as your only fertilizer? Not many!'

A look at the Lawn Institute's current website substantiates Mr Shery's contention. Half a million people work in the turfgrass industry. Total spending on professional landscaping, lawn care and tree care is running at fourteen billion dollars a year and rising. A fifth of homeowners, twenty-two million of them, hire such help. Spending on lawn care amounts to one third of the gardening budget. The Lawn Institute shows itself aware that a concern for the environment has become an accepted feature of middle-class America's social awareness, and makes the necessary adjustments to the message. Turf is hailed as 'an environmental hero', on the grounds that the lawn supposedly provides one person's daily oxygen intake, helps cool the air, controls allergy-provoking dust and pollen, absorbs pollutants like carbon dioxide, nationally neutralizes twelve million tons of floating dust and dirt, filters water into groundwater supplies, acts as a buffer against pesticides, is a larder for birds and insects and prevents soil erosion.

So, the mantra goes, the lawn is good for our world, good for our health, good for us and for our children. But most of all, it is good for our property values. The Lawn Institute makes much of a Gallup poll defining the five perceived cardinal qualities:

1) Helps beautify the neighbourhood.
2) A place of beauty and relaxation for family, employees and visitors.
3) Reflects positively on owner.
4) Place of comfort for work and entertainment.
5) Adds to real estate value.

'Attractive lawns', the Institute says, 'offer curbside appeal, which prompts potential home buyers to visit the inside of the home ... Grass is perennial, so lawns are very durable investments.'

In the face of such an accretion of virtues, the sceptics face an uphill battle. Too many popular aspirations, beliefs, superstitions and misconceptions are synthesized in the lawn for its status as an institution to be genuinely vulnerable. How can you argue effectively against something which looks nice, provides exercise and jobs, helps keep you and those dear to you and the world at large healthy – and enhances the value of your home? The combination is irresistible.

Then and Now –
Greensward and
Minimum Bovver

*I am not a lover of lawns. Rather would I see daisies in
their thousands, ground ivy, hawkweed, and even the
hated plantain with tall stems, and dandelions with
splendid flowers and fairy down, than the too well-tended
lawn*

W.H. HUDSON

Assaults such as Hudson's did nothing to undermine the ascendancy which the lawn continued
to enjoy as the serene assumptions of Victorian England
merged into those of the Edwardian Age. Hudson saw
his spiritual territory – the ancient downland, woodland
and sweet valleys of England – threatened by the creeping spread of town and deadly, conforming suburbia.
But few shared his fears. Little disturbed the benign complacency with which the Englishman viewed his lawn,
and so much else. As he surveyed the world, contemplat-
ing how much of the best of it had the Union Jack flying
over it, he saw ample evidence to support the central
core of his belief: that in matters of climate, resources,
geographical placement, character and temperament,

his country and its people had been uniquely favoured.

In the matter of grass, the assumption was absolute. It was expressed in typical fashion in Reginald Blomfield's *The Formal Garden in England*, published not long before the end of the 19th century: 'The turf of an English garden is probably the most perfect in the world; certainly it is far more beautiful than any to be found on the Continent.'

Wrapped in their thick quilt of superiority, the British had no appetite for the missionary zeal taking root in America, nor did they feel any need to question the methods and traditions which served them so well. Grass seed mixtures remained much as they had been in Mrs Loudon's day, and Mr Lamson-Scribner's doctrine of racial purity never caught on. Instructions on how to lay down a lawn were faithful to the precepts stated by John James three centuries before. Writers tended to concern themselves with the impression of it, rather than the technicalities of it. Walter Godfrey addressed himself to the matter in his *Gardens in the Making*, which was published in 1914 (with a dedication to Mrs Illingworth Illingworth):

> Green turf is the carpet with which we lay the broad spaces of our garden floor. Its presence near the house is one of the most essential conditions of a beautiful and reposeful plan. The grass path is a thing of quite unrivalled charm. It must be kept in the very pink of condition, soft and with the springiness of velvet, with edges trimmed with unerring straightness . . .

There was no need for Godfrey to tell Mrs Illingworth Illingworth how to achieve these effects. This could be safely left to our rain, softer and more nourishing than anyone else's; our breezes, gentler and more beneficial; our sun, warming but never scorching; our mowers, the first, the best; and assorted sweating labourers, marshalled by a dependable head gardener, all reliant upon Mrs Illingworth Illingworth for shelter and the means to sustain existence.

Until the Great War, labour was cheap and readily available, and most of the gardening toil was done by paid help. The owner of the suburban residence or his wife might, if they were at all artistically inclined, organize the design, and lend a hand with some of the more agreeable tasks, pruning the roses, perhaps, or a spot of mowing. But it would not have occurred to them, any more than it would have done to the proprietors of the great country houses, to do other than leave the slog to the natural-born sloggers. Kipling made rough fun of this division in his poem 'The Glory Of The Garden':

> Our England is a garden that is full of stately views
> Of borders, beds and shrubberies and lawns and
>   avenues,
> With statues on the terraces and peacocks strutting
>   by;
> But the Glory of the Garden lies in more than
>   meets the eye.
>
> Our England is a garden, and such gardens are
>   not made
> By singing 'Oh how beautiful' and sitting in the
>   shade,
> While better men than we go out and start their
>   working lives
> At grubbing weeds from gravel paths with broken
>   dinner knives.

Then seek your job with thankfulness and work till
    further orders,
If it's only netting strawberries or killing slugs on
    borders.
And when your back stops aching and your hands
    begin to harden
You will find yourself a partner in the Glory of the
    Garden.

Oh Adam was a gardener, and God who made
    him sees
That half a proper gardener's work is done upon
    his knees.
So when your work is finished, you can wash your
    hands and pray
For the Glory of the Garden that it may not pass
    away!
And the Glory of the Garden it shall never pass
    away.

In Edwardian England, the idea of a member of the
land-owning classes with an aching back, dirty knees or
earth lodged beneath broken fingernails was unimaginable. The Englishman was still accustomed to stand at
his drawing room window, look out over his terrace,
his grass tennis court, his croquet lawn, the greensward
around and about, the shrubberies and borders and
stands of great trees, enclosed in thick, ivy-clad walls, and
feel much as the Squire in Trollope's *The Small House at
Allington* had felt.

It is true that the social upheaval accompanying the
Great War swept much of that old world away. The idyll
pictured by Henry James, in which impossibly gracious
members of the idle aristocracy disported themselves on
sweeping lawns of infinite softness dating back to Crom-
well's time, nattering of love and literature, while the

great unwashed went about its obscure, sordid business beyond the estate walls, could no longer be sustained. Too many people had died, too many lives had been shattered, too many of the survivors could testify to the horrors that mankind has visited upon itself. And, in practical terms, cheap labour was no longer available to keep those great gardens going.

On the other hand, the years of war did nothing to undermine the British passion for the garden, or the place of the lawn within it. If anything, the experience of conflict had intensified the yearning for the tranquillity and innocence which the garden symbolized. The garden, almost alone, had been unpolluted by the slaughter, devastation and cruelty. The trees and shrubs had matured, the flowers had bloomed, the lawns – well, at least they had not been laid waste. All was still there, looking a little ragged perhaps, but needing no more than care and attention to be restored to full health. Consolation and comfort were there, and with them a link, a spiritual chain, leading from the uncertain present to that previous, secure world.

Shortly after the war ended, a four-volume treatise, *Practical Gardening for Pleasure and Profit*, was published, under the editorship of a Mr W. Wright. He revelled in the supremacy of our turf:

> Famed far beyond the confines of our tight little island are the lawns of England. Visitors from overseas look on these smooth swards of velvet verdure, and covet and admire. Sometimes, in order to keep in colour with the grass, they turn green – with envy.

One can imagine Mr Wright chuckling with delight at this extraordinarily feeble joke. The core of his beliefs was clearly formed in sun-kissed Edwardian days. But the experience of war inspired him to tack on a new, more democratic vision, of the British as a 'nation of gardeners'. 'What does this mean?' he asks himself:

> It means that the spectre of starvation has no terrors for us. Denial of luxury – yes! Restriction of titbits – perhaps! Actual want – no! It means health . . . it means education – not the pseudo-education of the schools but the true education which is based on the solid ground of nature . . . A nation of gardeners, then, is a nation of patriots . . . It is a virile, active, energetic nation. It has a sound mind in a sound body.

And that, Mr Wright might have added, means that, just as we lead the world in cultivating lawns, flowers and vegetables, so – when we are roused – do we administer a good thrashing on the battlefield to races inferior by reason of their exclusion from these character-forming blessings.

The post-war shortage of labour strengthened the grip on the public consciousness of the principle that no British garden was complete – or, indeed, was a garden at all – without a decent lawn. With the ranks of the labouring classes so thinned, many owners found themselves compelled to grass over areas of their gardens previously devoted to borders. Steady advances in mowing technology assisted the process. Although Ransomes had introduced the motor mower as long ago as 1902, in the early years it was available only in sizes suitable for sports grounds or great estates, and up to 1914 no more than six hundred had been sold. Gradually, petrol-driven mowers became more manageable and widely used – although the push mower retained its pre-eminent position in the market, and pony power continued to be exploited. Two factors which held back the growth in motor mowing were the high cost of the machines – in 1925 the Shanks 42-incher retailed at £335, the 35-incher at £280 – and their weight. Even a mower with 24-inch cutters weighed several hundredweight.

Other makers entered the market to dispute with Ransomes, Green and Shanks – among them Dennis Brothers of Guildford, Charles H. Pugh of Birmingham (the 'Atco') and JP Engineering of Leicester. As production increased – in 1928 JP sold more than twelve thousand machines – costs came down steeply. In 1930 the standard Atco 22-inch model was priced at £75, and by the mid-1930s Qualcast's cheapest mower was less than £15.

Little by little, a more rigorous attitude to grass itself developed. The tolerance, indeed affection, of men like Shirley Hibberd for moss and clover gave way to a more exclusive identification of what did, and did not, properly belong in the well-tended lawn. In H. H. Thomas's 1925 textbook, *The Complete Amateur Gardener*, clover was still permitted, but moss and daisies had become unwelcome intruders, to be suppressed by the use of lawn sand. The casts left by the garden's universal and indefatigable resident, the earthworm, were also regarded as a blot on the lawn's pure visage. Thomas suggested that, in moderation, they needed merely to be swept away. But where they abounded, worm killer was called for.

In 1931 the first book to be devoted exclusively to

grass culture, Reginald Beale's *The Book of the Lawn*, was published. It displays a distinct hardening in attitude. Its tone is authoritarian and illiberal, and its message is couched in terms infected with competitive and militaristic imagery. The lawn is seen as an arena for manly contest, or as a battlefield. The steps in its creation are described as the England cricket captain might present his plan for defeating the Australians, or a platoon commander his strategy for an impending offensive. Once the basics have been done – the site levelled, drained, cleared of stones and weeds, raked, sown, raked again, rolled, mowed, spiked, patched, and fertilized – attention is turned to the enemy.

Beale's tactics owe more than a little to the lessons of the Great War. There is no place here for gentlemanliness, chivalry or generosity towards the adversary. The victor will be the one whose troops are the most thoroughly prepared, whose armaments are the most advanced and effective, whose vigilance is the most constant, and whose pursuit of the goal is the most ruthless.

The enemies are various and resourceful. Chief among the weeds is the common plantain, though the daisy is 'one of the worst'. 'It is essential', Beale urges ,'for the owner of a lawn to fight the weeds year in and year out . . . unless they are killed, they will win the battle.' But you may not relax, even when the weeds are routed. They have allies, even more pernicious. There are moles, which must be gassed, using Brocks Port Fire. Ant nests must be opened and drenched – at whatever hazard to the lawn-keeper – with carbon disulphide, which is 'highly inflammable and consequently dangerous'. The weapon against the vile leatherjacket – the grub of the daddy-longlegs, whose speciality is producing patches of brown, dead grass – is Kil-Jac, an application of which will leave the treated area 'literally smothered in dead and dying grubs'.

But of all the lawn's foes, one is to be feared and hated above all others:

> Of the pests that attack turf the earthworm takes the premier position and undoubtedly does more damage than all the rest put together . . . The damage they do to mowing machines is beyond belief . . . they foul the turf . . . their slimy casts make wonderful seedbeds for weeds.

There is, the commander cries, but one way to combat such a pestilence: Worm Killer, and plenty of it.

> The worms, large and small, struggle to the surface in thousands to die . . . the Worm Killer is absolutely infallible.

The drawback with lawn war, as opposed to human war, is that it cannot be pursued to total victory. Had a means been available to Reginald Beale to extirpate the worms and their allies, I suspect he would have taken it. As it is, the best the successful leader can hope for is to stay on top, depriving the other side of the means to regroup, ready to resume severe offensive operations if the circumstances demand. Beale remembered only too well what could happen if things were allowed to slide. On his own lawn, the Great War interrupted what had been twenty years of attritional control. While guns blazed and men perished on the battlefields of France, at home 'the weeds won the game'.

Mowing was, of course, the primary means of keeping the upper hand in this continuous antagonism. The man responsible for it was like a prison governor, or the commanding officer of a garrison in conquered territory. For him, mowing was not a pleasant way to unwind after a busy week in the office. It was akin to going on manoeuvres, or laying a minefield, or strengthening fortifications:

> On no account should the grass be allowed to grow over one inch long . . . The moment it is allowed to do so, it begins to deteriorate . . . The old-fashioned idea, prompted by laziness and ignorance, of putting the mower away between October and March, cannot be deprecated too seriously.

Sandwiched between Reginald Beale's outbursts of martial fervour were slabs of perfectly sound advice on making and maintaining a lawn; and one suspects that most readers would have applied as much of that as they could be bothered with, and ignored the rhetoric. By the mid-1930s the means to achieve a decent lawn were easily and cheaply available. Sound scientific study was being carried out at the Bingley research centre near Bradford, which had been established in 1929, to produce advice on seed mixtures, fertilizers, weed treatments and the like. It was up to the gardener whether he or she wished to aspire to the velvet greensward, or was content with an expanse of imperfect, hard-wearing, pleasing turf. The evangelical message promoted so energetically in the United States secured few converts in Britain. With God, the British climate and the unsurpassable expertise of the British engineer on his side, the British gardener had no need of it.

So secure had the lawn become in the scheme of things since the time of Shirley Hibberd that later generations of designers and writers largely lost interest in it. Every concept began with a lawn, but there was nothing to say about it. Excitement and originality were provoked by more testing matters: of proportion and arrangement, the use and abuse of colour, the reconciliation of past and present, the exploitation of new hybrid varieties and the new species brought from China and Tibet. To be sure, there was grass within the Sackville-West gardens at Sissinghurst, and at Miss Jekyll's Mumstead Wood; but the ladies hardly bothered to say how it got there. There was grass, perfect grass, spread around Sir Philip Sassoon's paradise at Port Lympne; but it was no more than a backdrop, filling in the spaces between the flower-dense borders, the glistening fountain pool, the clipped yew hedges, the great stone staircase and the other elements in his rich and gorgeous conception.

As in America, the Second World War interrupted the march of the lawn. Many gardeners responded to the call to help feed the nation by digging up their lovingly cherished pieces of turf and converting them to vegetable plots. But with peace restored, the lawn quickly resumed its place as the garden's *sine qua non*. As home ownership expanded, so did lawns multiply. Broadly speaking, people in Britain did not have to be convinced that the garden which came with their house should contain a lawn. They merely wished to be told how to do it.

Consequently, the blandishments of the British lawn care industry seem remarkably pallid, compared with the loud assertions of its American equivalent. An issue of the *Gardener's Chronicle* of 1960 contains advertisements on behalf of four British mower manufacturers. The Atco is a 'motor mower for life'. The Green 'gives every lawn a close, even cut – a bowling green finish'. The Suffolk Punch is 'unbeatable'. The Qualcast Super Panther has 'sleek thoroughbred lines ... looks bliss to use, proves bliss to use'. How restrained, how quaint, how so, so terribly English these encomiums are! There are no rousing military images, exhortations to conquer, control and exterminate, vulgar references to enhanced property values, no aggressive invocation of a male-dominated society. The implication behind these polite endorsements is that the British gardener does not need to be told what he needs the machine for, any more than he needs to be told that mowing is man's work; and that he would be embarrassed by an appeal to him to assert his masculinity. The mowers are introduced as if they were candidates in a Parliamentary election. We know that they are good chaps and incapable of anything other than fair play; and merely wish to be informed about the specifications of the engine, the nature of the starting mechanism, the means by which the height of the cut can be adjusted.

The industry flourished. In 1954 Ransomes sold more than forty-two thousand push mowers, almost ten thousand motor mowers, and more than a thousand of the gang mowers which had been developed in the United States for cutting golf fairways, and had become widely used on sports grounds and recreation fields. The ancient names of Green and Shanks survived, but in increasingly precarious competition with other more innovative and energetic manufacturers. The first rotary mowers had been developed in the 1930s, and the Shay Rotoscythe became extremely popular because of its ability to cope with long, rough grass to which the traditional cylinder machine was unsuited. The rotary principle was refined by companies like Hayter and Mountfield, and began to challenge the dominance of the traditional cylinder design.

In 1963 Flymo introduced the brainchild of the Swedish designer, Karl Dahlman. It was a rotary mower in which the cutter revolved over a cushion of air, and it revolutionized the practise of grass-cutting and the attitudes associated with it. The primary asset of the hover mower had nothing whatever to do with the quality of the finish it produced. Indeed, its triumph in the market place depended on consigning that notion to the steadily growing scrap heap of similarly redundant traditional values. This was the dawning of the age in which the white heat of technological advance would confer on the societies which embraced it an unimaginable abundance of leisure and comfort, liberating the new generation from those outmoded conventions which had so constricted the lives of their parents; among which the practice of expending several hours manhandling a weighty piece of metal up and down an expanse of grass until its shaven and striped demeanour corresponded with the accepted norm of excellence was but one.

The Flymo was cheap, light, as easy to manoeuvre as a toothbrush. The essence of its attractiveness – convenience – was in perfect harmony with the spirit of the times. All it lacked was the slogan, to light its fire. In a way, the genius which inspired 'It's a Lot Less Bovver With a Hovver' was even more in tune with the age than

Karl Dahlmann's invention itself. Propelled by that bewitching ditty, the Flymo swept all before it, banishing the old 'velvet sward' ideal to the dustbin labelled sentimental, useless clutter of the past; where it joined bowler hats, steam engines, starched collars, suet puddings, split-cane fishing rods, cricket bats which needed oiling, English seaside holidays and much else besides.

Within a decade the 'less bovver' principle embodied in the Flymo had established dominance in the mass market. But competition being what it is, the product itself was challenged all the way, chiefly by Qualcast. Qualcast's rival to the Flymo was its Concorde, a cheap, basic, mains-driven cylinder mower. The battle between them became one, not of their respective merits as pieces of grass-cutting machinery, but of the slogans. Here Qualcast resorted to means foul or brilliant, according to the perspective. 'A Lot Less Bovver With a Hovver' became 'A Lot Less Bovver Than a Hovver', a minimalist verbal adjustment exposing a world of difference. It enabled Qualcast to scrap with the orange champion on something approaching level terms, until the moment the hover patent expired, whereupon Qualcast leaped aboard the bandwagon.

Other factors were at work, helping elbow the traditional striped lawn and its attendant petrol and push mowers to the margins. As pressure upon building land intensified, and outlets for leisure multiplied, so did lawns shrink. By 1989 more than one third of Britain's sixteen million or so lawns were smaller than thirty-eight square yards, and a mere tenth covered a hundred square yards or more. Increasingly, home-owners found that they did not want anything more from the patch of coarse grass, moss and weeds which they called the lawn than that their children should be able to play football on it, and that it should be passably tidy. And they found that the small, light, cheap, easily maintained, mass-produced grass-cutter answered well enough.

No longer valued, most of the great names of mower craftsmanship perished. Green, Shanks, Webb, JP, vanished. Ransomes bid farewell to the domestic garden to concentrate on the golf course and sports field market, and marked its bicentenary by falling into American ownership. Dennis disappeared from Guildford. Among the smaller companies, Alletts of Arbroath has survived, as has Lloyds of Letchworth still producing its incomparable Paladin. The market today is ruled by a handful of mass producers: Qualcast-Atco (part of the Robert Bosch Group), Black and Decker, Honda and Flymo.

Against such a background, it is clear any notion that a majority of British householders share a passion for, or enthusiasm for, or indeed lively interest in, the lawn is unsustainable. But nor, statistically, are we a nation of gardeners – as we are undoubtedly a nation of super-market shoppers, car owners and television watchers. The majority of the residents in the village where I live – a large, straggling, wholly unpicturesque Home Counties settlement – are not gardeners in any meaningful sense. The plots in which the majority of the houses stand are not gardens, but spaces. There may be a few mediocre shrubs struggling for life in the impoverished sub-soil with which the developer cloaked his discarded rubble and rubbish; a straggly tree or two of unknown species; a weed-stuffed strip which was once a flower bed. And there is grass, which the home-owner – preferring not to confront a wilderness when he steps outside the door and having no clue what else he might do with the space – cuts with a cheap motor mower when the mood takes him or the pressure becomes irresistible. He has no affection for the stuff, nor concern for its welfare.

So, no, we are not a nation of lawn lovers or gardeners. But nor should the scale of the triumph of the 'minimum bovver' principle be exaggerated. Alongside the great majority of the uninterested, there are the four, five, six million of us who – while not necessarily calling ourselves gardeners – would own up to a curiosity about and active involvement in some aspect of what goes on in the place we call the garden. For the majority among this considerable constituency, the care of the lawn would probably be regarded in neutral terms, as one of a number of necessary tasks, or as a bothersome chore. But there is a considerable minority in whom cultivated grass arouses emotions ranging from mild affection through warm enthusiasm to consuming passion. To see them, you must go to the gardening centre in spring, as their grass comes to life. They will be surveying the shelves of weed exterminators, humping sacks of moss-killer and fertilizer, scrutinizing the beguiling promises on boxes of seed, looking longingly at the ranks of glistening green mowers, thumbing attentively through the pages of manuals of instruction. The size of the minority is a matter of speculation. But it is big enough to justify garden centres devoting more space to lawn care products than to any other branch of the pastime. Gather them together, and they would make an impressive army of consumers.

*

Forty years and more ago, Marjery Fish wrote in her classic account of a horticultural love affair, *We Made a Garden*: 'The four essentials of a good garden are perfect lawns, paths, hedges and walls.' And she observed of her husband and partner: 'Walter would no more have left his grass uncut or his edges untrimmed than he would have neglected to shave.' Standards have certainly slipped since those innocent days – I myself sometimes do the mowing unshaven. But, in the mightily conservative, tradition-heavy world of the British garden, the place of Marjery Fish's fundamentals has remained pretty secure; that of the lawn wholly so. Most people in charge of anything bigger than the smallest town or cottage garden simply cannot imagine it without cultivated grass. The lawn is as essential to the garden as the roof to the house.

Efforts to dislodge it from its position of eminence have proved largely futile. Bleatings about the supposed tyranny it exercises from time to time escape the writers and designers, who are fond of calling it a shibboleth. A more concentrated anti-lawn movement arose a few years ago, inspired by the droughts of the late 1980s and early 1990s, which made most expanses of grass look as if they had been attacked with a flame-thrower. With verdant velvet transformed into crisp beige, and the airwaves alive with nonsense about the coming of Britain's 'Mediterranean-style climate', the country's favourite ground cover seemed briefly under threat. At least one of the big water companies suggested that customers distressed by the condition of their lawns should dig them up, and replace them with artificial grass. Daring gardening journalists suggested paving or coloured chippings, or a wild flower meadow better able to retain moisture. Mower sales declined – partly because parched brown lawns do not require mowing. 'Is the great British love affair with the lawn over?' one or two provocative scribes asked. A couple of damp summers, green as of old, provided the answer.

Gardening, like cooking, exists on two planes: one largely fabulous, the other more or less real. The first is inhabited by professionals – chattering television presenters, wacky designers, plantsmen and plantswomen steeped in botanical Latin, newspaper columnists skilled in the art of dressing up as new the same old wisdom that they've been dishing out at the same time each season since the year dot. The second is occupied by the garden outside the back door, with its stony, lumpy soil, its rampant ground elder and couch grass, its unweeded borders, its unpruned, diseased, clapped-out rose bushes, its aphid-ravaged raspberries, caterpillar-chewed gooseberries and slug-wasted brassicas; the evidence it presents in every corner of neglect mitigated by short-lived bursts of activity.

The great army of practical gardeners will dabble in the first plane. They will skim the gardening pages in the newspapers, watch the TV programmes, nod with interest when the experts whose livelihoods depend on having something 'lively' and 'provocative' to say advocate replacing the tedious lawn with pond, patio or the current favourite flavour, wood decking. They may visit famous gardens, or go to Chelsea, and come back with an idea or two: put in a fountain, install a pergola, make an arbour.

Then they return to the real garden, where the season

189

begins with a tremendous burst of zeal and a series of expensive sorties to gardening centres and nurseries, and ends with a list as long as your arm of things done wrong, half-done and left undone, and yet another resolution that all will be different next year; where the tedious lawn is not dug up, because the reality of what would go in its place is no reality at all. In the real garden, the real gardener – short of time, money and creative imagination – needs, not a load of half-digested fancy stuff from a smart-arsed television celebrity, but sound advice from a trusted source firmly located in the real world. Just as our forebears got it from John James of Greenwich, so do we get it in the books of the wholly untelevisual, totally real Doctor David Hessayon.

The Hessayon phenomenon – measured in the most obvious fashion by the staggering sales of his gardening manuals – provides a revealing insight into what actually goes on in the ordinary gardens of Britain. The Doctor does not share a gardening world with Beth Chatto, Stephen Lacey and Roy Lancaster, or even Alan Titchmarsh and the late Geoff Hamilton. His garden is as far removed from theirs as the typical suburban home is from Vita Sackville-West's Sissinghurst or Christopher Lloyd's Great Dixter.

Doctor Hessayon's literary ability is non-existent, his style is reminiscent of that of a conscientious A-level student. His voice is like that of the man who runs the local ironmonger's, flat and dull. But if you take the trouble to listen, you will get the information you need. Even if he were capable of pretentiousness, of frills, of flights of the imagination (which one strongly doubts), Doctor Hessayon would repudiate them. His mission is information. His genius is to apprehend the scale of the division between fancy and reality, and to retail his wares in the world of the real garden.

The Hessayon concept begins with the lawn. One suspects that he could no more imagine a garden without a lawn than himself leaving his house without his trousers on. When his manual on lawn care first appeared, in the mid-1960s, it was called *Be Your Own Lawn Expert*, and cost two-and-sixpence. In its most recent incarnation, it is entitled *The New Lawn Expert* and costs just under six pounds. The use of the word 'new' is deceptive. Its increased size is largely accounted for by a more extravagant use of illustration, by some introductory words extolling Britain as 'the home of the Beautiful Lawn' and the virtues of the Hessayon approach in keeping it that way, and two additional chapters – one dealing with the history of the lawn, the other consisting of a succession of tepid nods in the direction of alternatives to the lawn ('much is written these days about the wild flower meadow . . . in reality this form of ground cover is difficult to create and even more difficult to maintain'). The section dealing with 'Lawn Troubles' is also considerably expanded, on the principle that the more we know about our enemies, the more efficiently we may dispose of them.

In essence, though, the word according to Doctor Hessayon has not changed in thirty years. He opens by defining the grades of lawn, in the way that the manager of a tailor's might display the various classes of cloth. At the top comes the first-rate lawn (luxury grade), exclusively of bents and fescues, to be 'seen by all but walked on by very few'. Beneath that come the first-rate lawn (utility grade), with ryegrass and broad-leaved grasses predominant – 'for living on rather than just looking at'; the second-rate lawn, afflicted by various failings but capable of being nursed back to health; and finally the worn-out lawn, consisting of moss, weeds and bare earth, and beyond redemption.

The fundamentals of the programme for the care of the lawn are unvaried: mowing, raking, spiking, top dressing, fertilizer application, edge trimming, moss, weed and pest extermination. There are occasional variations in detail between early and contemporary Hessayon (mysteriously, the fertilizer spreader is relegated from being an essential in 1967 to being an extra in 1999, while the 'straight plank' – to check for bumps and hollows – leaps from nowhere into the indispensable category). But on the great issues, Hessayon has not changed his mind – on watering, for instance. To him, a lawn the colour of a biscuit is no lawn at all. Unmoved by cries for conservation, unaffected by any doubt about the sense of lavishing thousands of gallons of water on a plant which is exceptional in its reluctance to die of thirst, the Doctor tells his disciples that at the first sign of trouble – which he identifies as a loss of 'springiness' – they must start watering thoroughly; and continue to do so until such time as rain comes to their aid, or the water companies indulge their 'maddening habit' of enforcing a hose-pipe ban.

When it comes to what he coyly calls 'Lawn Troubles', Doctor Hessayon's imperviousness to environmental concerns and concepts of correctness is even more striking.

Weeds are 'plants growing in the wrong place . . . that means any plant which is not a variety of grass recommended for turf cultivation'. Such plants must be persuaded to refrain from reproduction and absent themselves, or be destroyed with a systemic weedkiller. On the subject of pests, the doctor has become more intolerant with age. In the sixties, the enemies were two in number: earthworms and ants. But by the turn of the millennium their ranks had swelled to include leatherjackets ('the worst of all insect pests'), chafer grubs, moles ('one of the saddest sights in gardening is to see a fine, even lawn suddenly ruined by moles'), birds ('sparrows can be a problem on newly seeded lawns') and bitches ('dogs are no respecters of lawns').

The earthworm remains at the top of the list. Hessayon dismisses the case presented by the creature's defenders – 'they are supposed to have a beneficial effect by producing drainage holes within the soil . . . the harm caused by the mounds of coiled sticky earth which they produce far outweighs any benefits'. He rues the day that most efficient worm destroyer, chlordane, was outlawed, which has reduced the worm-hating lawn-lover to brushing away the casts with a besom and applying lawn sand. The Doctor refrains from calling for the execution of marauding bitches, noting with resignation that there are 'no effective repellents'. But grubs and ants are simply begging to be subjected to chemical attack, while there can be no sentimentality in dealing with the mole – 'moles tend to return if they are not killed . . . poisoning is the alternative method of killing moles'.

It is not difficult to mock the doctor, to laugh at him for his intolerance and dogmatism, his primitive English style, his allegiance to the doctrine of the lawn's racial purity, his disdain for experts and is comically dreary ideas about garden design; to see him as a dim, suburban spokesman on behalf of the horti-chemical industry. That is to miss the point, which is that he is right. The Word of Hessayon is utterly sound. An alliance between the climate of the British Isles and careful adherence to his instructions will produce the Beautiful Lawn.

The doctor's great gift is that he speaks to Everyman: the man who is quite content with the mediocre, the man who aspires a little higher, the man whose soul is moved by a true passion for grass. Unlike so many self-appointed authorities, he does not attempt to deceive his public by disguising the unattainable as the commonplace. He tells it as it is: that what you get depends on how much you are prepared to put in. He apprehends a significant truth, which is that the lawn requires no talent, no flair. It is quite unlike other elements of the garden. There is no individuality to it, no need for 'green fingers'. It is, quite simply, a matter of committing the effort and expenditure that the various steps in the programme require, and performing the specified functions in the right order, at the right time. The extent to which the lawn owner commits himself determines the quality of his lawn. It is prosaic, and obvious, and boring: and three and a quarter million copies of Doctor Hessayon's lawn manual are powerful evidence of how dearly we cherish those qualities.

MUSINGS
FROM THE SHED
(2)

Lawn Order,
Man's Business

One man went to mow.
Went to mow a meadow . . .

It would have to be a man. No one would write a poem or song, however absurd and repetitive, about a woman mowing anything. That is not to say that women have not mown meadows and lawns, and don't; merely that there is nothing to celebrate or remark upon when they do. My mother, who is eighty-five, cuts her patch of front lawn with a tiny, mains-driven machine which can be lifted with one hand. She does it, but she does not expatiate on the subject, which I own I occasionally do. The affinity between the male and mowing – whether scything hay or cutting cultivated grass – is set in stone.

Where lawns are concerned, it is also perceived as an Anglo-Saxon peculiarity. Lawns are, of course, grown, maintained and held dear across the world; but, for cultural and climatic reasons, the passion for the sward is grouped by the world into the corpus of English idiosyncrasies. There is a scene in one of the Asterix books in which the hero, pursued in his cart by a Roman patrol, takes off from the straight road across country. In his path is the lawn of an ancient Briton, on the edge of which stands his thatched cottage. The Englishman, a ludicrous caricature in handlebar moustaches, waistcoat and breeches, is seen contentedly emptying his watering can over the sward. He bends to behead an aberrant dandelion, murmuring: 'Another two thousand years of loving care, and I think it'll make quite a decent bit of turf.' 'Oh, I say,' he expostulates as Asterix's cart gouges trenches across his pride and joy, 'that's a bit off.' The pursuing Romans arrive, and the Englishman's slowly aroused dander is up. 'Here, I say, sir, please keep off the grass,' he protests. The centurion bellows at him to let the emissaries of Rome pass, but the Englishman will not budge: 'My garden is smaller than your Rome, but my pilum is harder than your sternum,' he ripostes, jabbing his spear into the centurion's midriff.

Mowing, then, is man's work. Historically, this may be explained by the physical demands. But the gender division goes much deeper than mere ease of use. For the male, there is something symbolically fulfilling in it; as there is in, say, cleaning a car. Women do, of course, clean cars, but the performance is unlikely to be tinged with ritualistic significance. For many male owners, the car fulfils the role of hunting trophy – useful, like meat, but more than that: a symbol of power and success.

Research carried out in the United States illustrates the different way in which men and women view the garden. Put simplistically, women tend to have a wider apprehension of the idea of 'home', in which the dwelling and its garden belong to each other, and are enhanced by each other. Just as the rooms, while discharging various and particular functions, contribute to the whole, so does the garden. And the garden itself is seen as an integrated, personal micro-environment, whose heterogeneous elements are – or should be – in harmony with each other, dependent upon each other, complementing each other.

For the female gardener, the lawn is no more than one constituent of the whole, and one of the least interesting. She sees the grass in relation to what is around it, or enclosed by it – shrubs, flower beds, trees, terrace, pond, bird bath, and so on. If necessary, she will give it time and effort, but only as much as is necessary for it to play its part in the overall scheme. Of itself, it is a bore and a chore; and if someone else, whether for money or for some impenetrable motive, can be persuaded to take it off her hands, so much the better.

For the male – domesticated hunter-gatherer and demobilized warrior – the garden is separate from the house, its character entirely distinct. It represents his old adversary, Nature, annexed and subjugated; but with its genetic links to wilderness origins still intact, and therefore still capable of resistance and even – if left to itself – reversion. It comprises an assortment of challenges to his assumption of control. There are trees to be kept in order, hedges to be clipped, mounds of rubbish to be burned or turned into useful compost, paths to be laid, fences to be put up, greenhouses and sheds to be assembled and maintained: a whole system of symbols of Man's civilizing authority. Of these symbols, the lawn is perhaps the most satisfying, and most cherished.

The appeal of the lawn to the conventional masculine temperament is rich and many-layered. It is a province of its own, its distinctness defined by its clean-edged boundaries. It requires specialized instruments to keep it in order, specialized foods and tonics to keep it healthy. Because of the way grass grows, its care is highly congenial to the repetitive rituals with which men like to organize their lives. The lawn is like a dog which must, come what may, be exercised. It is dependent on its carer, and that dependence quietly nourishes his ego. Like his wife and children, the lawn demands his protection. But, unlike them, it does not strike back; and, unlike them, it responds reliably to his love and attention.

Although the lawn co-exists with flower beds, to the lawnsman this is no more than a sharing of space. In its nature it is as distinct as fish from fowl. Grass is uniform in colour, predictable in behaviour, needing no more than the careful observance of an unchanging routine to be kept healthy. In contrast, flowers are fickle and unreliable, their variations in colour and habit making them hostile to the notion of regularity. To prosper, they demand an almost mystical sympathy, which cannot be purchased from the garden centre, nor easily acquired from a manual of instruction. To the lawnsman, the flower bed is *terra incognita*, where a woman's intuitive sense permits her, and her only, to wander in safety.

Anyway, he has enough on his hands. For, to the role of faithful pet, the lawn adds that of model battlefield. It is under constant attack and threat from a host of invaders, insurgents and undercover agents. They lay siege from without, they nibble away at the body politic from within. Weed seeds parachute in from neighbouring fields of racially inferior meadow grass. Plantains, daisies and buttercups infiltrate the defences. Moss appears from God knows where. Leatherjacket grubs gnaw the tender roots, producing brown plague spots. Moles sneak in underground, rabbits overground. Earthworms by the million foul the turf with their slippery extrusions. Wandering cats crap and bitches spray their discolouring piss.

As he becomes aware of the range of his adversaries, the lawnsman with a properly developed sense of duty learns that his obligations extend far beyond the weekly mow. As the guardian, he must defend the lawn against those who would do it harm. True, he is but one; and they are many. But fortunately he is bigger, stronger, cleverer and more resourceful than they are. All he has to do is to descend on his local garden centre, help himself from the available stock of armaments and other aids, observe the instructions, and victory will be his.

To contain the weaponry and other necessities, the lawnsman has a command centre, which is his shed. This construction – however ramshackle and leaky it may be – performs another satisfying function, which is to provide him with a sanctum. Here he keeps the mower, and cleans, feeds and repairs it. On some sagging shelf are arranged an array of insecticides, herbicides and fungicides, for the shed is field hospital, too. On the floor are dumped sacks of seed and fertilizer, with accessories – sprinkler, spreader, sprayer and the rest – distributed around. The shed has its own smell, like incense and old candle smoke in a church. A man is never short of an excuse to visit his shed.

But I began to suspect that there might be more to the gender issue than this, deeper impulses at work. As a man, I was curious to discover what it was within me that answered to the lawn and the task of ministering to it; why no woman I had ever known or heard of could have cared less about it. I contacted Professor Michael Argyle, the distinguished social psychologist, to ask him. He thought it might have something to do with men liking and using machines at work, and transferring that bias to the garden – which had the additional attraction of permitting them the autonomy and freedom usually denied them by their bosses. He readily agreed that men – himself included – much preferred the destructive side of garden care to the creative. He said his instinctive response on encountering a man with a keen enthusiasm for flowers would be to assume he was homosexual.

I laughed heartily at what I presumed was a joke. However, another notable psychologist, Halla Beloff, told me that displaying interest in, and aptitude for, arranging flowers was one of the tried and tested ways of checking on sexual identity and orientation. She agreed with Professor Argyle on the correlation between work at the place of work, and work in the garden. My objection – that most working men had little to do with machines other than computers any more – turned out to be no objection at all. Professor Beloff pointed out that, according to their traditional roles, men should be driving noisy machines, wielding sharp implements and generally deploying their muscle power; and that being frustrated in this role-fulfilment made them all the more inclined to grasp some engine of destruction when they got in the garden.

But what about lawns and mowing, I wanted to know?

Professor Beloff laughed. Was I aware, she asked, of the phallic dimension to mowing? I wasn't. She explained: that the mower was a source and symbol of potency, held out throbbing and thrusting in front of the male at approximately groin level, demanding and securing entry to the world outside, and changing that world. I was stunned. Was this a fantastic example of the psychologist searching within the simple for the unbelievably complex, a piece of grist for the psychobabbling mill? But Professor Beloff seemed far too amiable and sensible to peddle nonsense. And, anyway, what explanation did I have to offer?

I had a thought. How, I asked the professor, could mowing the lawn be equated to vigorous sexual intercourse, the presentation of the mower to the garden with the brandishing of the erect penis, if it happened but once a week? No red-blooded male would acknowledge that he was moved by the impulse on so regular and infrequent a basis (putting aside, for the sake of the argument, any evidence that this is, indeed, the pattern of most sexual activity within marriage in our society).

Professor Beloff declined to be knocked off course. She asserted that the phallic substitute was merely one aspect of the positive image of the mower, and that it was held in balance by another – which was that the comparative infrequency of the activity inhibited it from becoming a household chore. Household chores, she explained, were performed by women, and tended, by their nature, to be daily: cooking, cleaning, looking after children, tidying. It was one more illustration of the way in which the labours arising from the human condition had been divided in favour of men. Would I, she wondered, be so keen on doing the mowing if it had to be done every day? I gave in.

Professor Beloff was an observer, rather than a campaigner. She admitted quite contentedly that she and her husband, another psychologist, corresponded precisely to the gender patterns. He did the mowing, and would not – she assumed – want her to do it. This suited her, as she had no interest in it, and was sufficiently occupied training plants and weeding.

I asked the wives of two fairly extreme examples of the lawn-mowing zealot how they viewed the passion. Each said she liked 'a good lawn', on condition that she had nothing to do with making it so. Neither had any interest whatever in grass culture. One said her husband wouldn't have considered letting her mow, because of the assumption – which she seemed to share – that she wouldn't be capable of getting the lines straight. The other said she had no desire at all to perform a task which was so noisy and dirty and energetic, and which required whoever did it to come to lunch with hands stinking of Swarfega. Both used the word 'harmless' to characterize the activity. Both commended it on the grounds that it was better than going to the pub, and that it could not be done in the pub. I did not have the nerve to ask either of them if it had crossed their minds that it might be a substitute for sex, and therefore probably worse than going to the pub.

By this stage I was feeling a trifle insecure in my allegiance to the lawn. Was it – far from being an innocent enthusiasm – a symptom of a sinister desire for sexual penetration and for furthering the cause of male domination? I felt I needed to talk to a kindred spirit – a man, of course, but one who might give me an alternative, more reassuring version of the lawnsman's compulsion. So I telephoned the novelist, Jim Crace, to ask him about his lawn.

Anyone who has read *Quarantine* or any of Crace's other novels will know that he does not shun the dark places; rather that they are his preferred territory, to be explored with prose like a diamond cutter. I had never met him, but I had read a newspaper profile of him which contained an admiring reference to the quality of his greensward. Over the telephone he established his credentials as a lawnsman at once, by insisting that his turf was in a poor way and that the hack who had praised it knew nothing of such matters. All he could see, he said, were the fallen apples, the patches of discolouring from a bitch's urine, the sprouting of plantains and the insidious spread of moss – all this being the kind of thing lawnsmen always say.

It had come, he explained, from his father, who had worked as a groundsman, tending cricket squares, bowling greens and grass tennis courts. His father had been jealous of his turf; so much so that, on seeing a glider pilot circling overhead looking for somewhere to land, he had distributed machinery across the mown expanses to persuade the fellow to put to earth somewhere else. Crace told me that at the age of seventeen, he had crashed the family car not far from home, and had been ordered by his mother to bring the dreadful news to his father, who was cutting the lawn. Covered in blood, the youth stammered out his confession. 'All right, all right,' his father replied. 'Now get off the grass.'

At the Crace home there were two lawns, front and back. The role of the front lawn, much the smaller, was as a statement of respectability, for only philanderers neglected their front lawns. It was at the back, away from passing eyes, that his father – Webb mower in hand – observed the full rituals. I asked if he had ever wondered about the origin of the impulse. Crace thought it sprang from a deeply imprinted desire to control and domesticate nature. It was, he agreed, a purely masculine province, legitimized by being distinct from housework. There was no sympathy between him and his wife on the matter, he said. To him, the edges of the lawn were of vital importance, requiring that he kneel and use a pair of scissors to preserve and enhance their sculpted precision. Yet she, partner in a perfect marriage, would put her foot on that edge and squash it down, in Crace's words 'totally unacceptable behaviour, divorceable'; and worse, abandon across the emerald sward little mounds of decomposing weeds and tools, blighting its complexion.

Crace talked more about his father; how the care of the lawn and the allotment had been stitched into his apprehension of the family and its shared life; how, when slowly dying, he had striven to continue in the discharge of those duties. Crace had watched, and when his father could no longer mow the grass, the son had taken charge. And here was one explanation – 'I started turning into my father.'

PART THREE

Competition with the "EASY" LAWN MOWER

EASY BABY MOWER AT 10 A.M.

40 INCH EASY BEATS THEM ALL.

Nº 2. HALF AN HOUR LATER

The Lawnsmen

*To insure the luxury of a 'velvet lawn' is, to speak gener-
ally, a most easy matter*

JAMES SHIRLEY HIBBERD

Armed with the gospel according to the good Doctor Hessayon, I went forth into battle, my mission
to transform the unkempt, weed-infested, moss-thick
patches at the front and to the back of our house into
orthodox lawns. I had attempted this sort of thing before,
but long ago. And I had forgotten two things: firstly, how
much time and effort is required to treat even the smallest expanse of ground; and, secondly, how many of
gardening's most tedious, wearying and repetitive tasks
are concentrated on the business of making a lawn. The
Doctor omits to mention that. I strongly suspect that he
left the toil to someone else.

I began on the front lawn. Here, for many years before
our purchase of the house, the grass had been engaged
in a hopeless battle against the moss, conducted in the
shadow of two towering conifer trees which prevented
any sunlight from penetrating. We had the trees cut
down, and I applied a solution of ferro-sulphate which
turned the moss from a vital green to a sinister black.

Then I took up a wire rake and attacked it. The curious thing about raking moss is that, however much you remove, however many barrowfuls of the soft, downy stuff that you consign to the bonfire, as much remains; until, having been over the same piece of ground five times, you discover that there can never have been any grass there in the first place because the moss has now gone and all that is left is bare, lacerated earth.

At the back, different problems presented different challenges. There was grass, albeit somewhat rough and weedy, which I left to its own devices in order to prepare for seeding two areas from which we had removed the tangled remains of ancient shrubbery. This clearance work had been done in a flush of enthusiasm some months earlier. Now, as I dug over the ground, I found that it had been incomplete. There was a mass of shallow roots left behind, pale in appearance, of a strange, elastic consistency. I assaulted them energetically, until I had reached the edge of the existing lawn. I found that these roots had no respect for such boundaries. They had crept off beneath the turf, the yellowish tentacles thrusting through the fibrous root system of the grass. Moreover, at various points far distant from where the original tree had stood, they had sent up suckers, like outposts left by a colonizing power. These were marked by little clumps of fern-like leaves, strikingly vigorous in their growth, considering their isolation from the extirpated mother tree.

As I pursued the tentacles through the grass, like a Jesuit of the Inquisition on the trail of an insidious heresy, I developed a righteous hatred of the plant. The emotion was far more powerful than the gardener's normal antipathy towards ground elder, ivy, moss and other endemic nuisances. I felt there was something horrible, almost obscene about this growth, its sneaky mode of operation, its irrepressible vitality. On my knees I wrestled with it, until what had previously been an expanse of admittedly mediocre lawn looked as if it had been invaded by an army of worm-starved badgers and hooligan moles; and as I did so, I invested my enemy with the quality of evil, and appointed myself as the agent of virtue.

I wanted to know my enemy, and so I described it to my mother, who knows most things about the plant world. She said it sounded like a sumach. I looked it up in the encyclopaedia, and there it was: *Rhus typhina*, the Stag's Horn Sumach. It was described as a popular ornamental tree, celebrated for the beauty of its reddened foliage in autumn. Beyond a passing reference to the wandering habits of its root system making it an unsuitable companion for a lawn, there was no hint of its wickedness. I watched the smoke rising from the tangled mound of its offspring on my bonfire, with the grim satisfaction of the Witchfinder General at a public burning.

It was time to prepare the ground for seeding – the work of an afternoon, I reckoned, or perhaps a day at most. So I dug over the ground again, removing a surprising quantity of lesser weeds, which took one afternoon. I levelled it as best I could by eye, and edged the patch with strips of wood to prevent encroachment, which took another. I then raked it about a thousand times with the metal-toothed rake, removed a ton or so of stones by hand, and finally stamped it firm, which took a week's worth of afternoons.

To me, it now looked ready. But a sudden guilt possessed me, for, amid all this activity, I had omitted to consult the gospel according to the Doctor. When I did so, I was seized with shame. I found that my adherence to the liturgy had been, at best, incomplete, while several stages regarded as essential to the creation of the Beautiful Lawn I had overlooked altogether. The levelling should have been organized with a system of pegs with lines painted on them, a seven-foot straight-edged board and a spirit level, whereas I had merely squinted at the site, thrown a few spadefuls of earth around, squinted again, distributed a bit more earth, until it 'looked about right'. I had entirely neglected to investigate the drainage situation, and had failed to 'work in at least twenty-eight pounds of lime-free sand per square yard when digging'. I had not applied Paraquat to destroy perennial weeds, nor did my strategy permit the necessary fallow period for any surviving weeds to reveal themselves, and be destroyed. Finally, I had shirked the dragging of the screed over the loosened surface to create the perfect tilth in which my seed might flourish.

In short, I had shown myself to be a most unworthy disciple. The pressing question was: should I, could I, mend my ways? Should what had been left undone continue to be left undone, or be done? In theory, it was not too late to start again. I knew, in my heart, that my besetting sins in gardening, as in all other aspects of home maintenance and improvement, were to start doing something before I was ready, to fail to do it properly, and to refuse to go back and do it again. And my punishment was to regret that I had ever thought of doing it in the first place. So I looked at that patch of earth, and studied the word of the Doctor, and looked at the earth again. And my heart failed me. I took up the box of grass seed, and I cast that seed upon the ground.

Down on the south coast, where the finger of the Beaulieu estuary pokes deep into the New Forest, I found a scattering of long, low, smart bungalows, discreetly half-hidden among the oaks and beeches. The road went nowhere, and vividly un-English ornamental pheasants pecked in peace at its side. The soil here is thin and acid. When Alan Andrews, retired master baker of Barnet, migrated here from north London, they told him he would not have to mow more than twice a year, so wretched and unprofitable was the struggle of grass to grow. And, indeed, all but one of the homes in this clearing in the forest stood on impoverished rashes of moss, scraggy tufts of grass and bare earth.

Mr Andrews was of a family to whom gardening and gardens mattered. His father was a passionate nurturer of blooms, ever anxious to best his neighbours for colour and luxuriance, commonly to be found at breakfast studying a volume concerning propagation or pruning. Gardening was an essential element of Alan Andrews's strategy for retirement. He could not imagine the one without the other. When he and his wife migrated from north London to their new house, he found that the area around it, referred to by the builders as its landscaped gardens, was no garden at all, but an expanse of dust and stones dropping away to the forest, into which a few dull and doomed shrubs had been hurriedly dropped.

He ordered top soil of the best quality, two hundred tons of it, and his new neighbours murmured their disapproval as the lorries bringing it roared up the private road they shared. Mr Andrews commanded that the slope be civilized into a brace of terraced flats, in each of which borders would enclose level lawns. The turf came and was unrolled and cut to shape; and the beds were mulched and manured; and the species of plants that Mr and Mrs Andrews liked and trusted were tenderly consigned to their ordained places.

Unlike his father, Alan Andrews had no need to compete with anyone, for no one around had ambitions to match his. Nor did he much care – or if he did, he kept it to himself – when, in that osmotic way so characteristic of communities of the retired and the retiring, it was made known to him that his concept of an Englishman's garden was considered rather 'suburban' for the sylvan setting. His spiraeas and his berberis, his brooms and hebes, his elaeagnus, escallonias and fuchsias, were all essential components in his mental picture of what he intended to be his last home. He was not minded to sacrifice them on the altar of provincial prejudice.

He was in his mid-seventies, a man of medium height, with a sliver of a silver moustache, a hearing aid and an evident enthusiasm for his life; Rotarian, church-goer, ex-village hall treasurer, contemptuous of those who would not bother to enter into the life of the little village of Beaulieu, perched beside the reedy waters of the estuary. As we strolled through the garden (there was no invitation to go inside, and why should there have been) he told me that he and Mrs Andrews did not care for weeds. Nor do I, but in my garden there are plenty. In

Mr Andrews's I scarcely saw one. The two lawns were as flat as tables, cut evenly but not short, the fine-leaved grass in easy ascendancy over the occasional dab of clover or daisy. But there were dark smears, trails of an invader. Mr Andrews and his wife do not care for wildlife any more than weeds, except the varieties that leave the garden alone. Deer and moles they dislike particularly; and these, unmistakeably, were the signs of molish questing for worms, as welcome to Mr Andrews as a dead mouse would have been in one of his loaves of bread. His wife, he told me as if it were the most normal thing in the world, would go out at night armed with a torch and a garden fork, and stab the creatures as they tunnelled. From this mild, courteous, godly man, this struck me as a little chilling.

Possibly in reaction to his father's enthusiasm for the blaze of colour, Mr Andrews's garden is a statement of sober, middle-class decency, a meticulously maintained, intricately ordered display of restrained harmony, the tropical burst of the bougainvillaea in the conservatory the one touch of the showman. He mows twice a week with his faithful Ransomes Marquis, applies fertilizer and weedkiller in the prescribed fashion, says with a little shrug that there's nothing much to it if you don't let things get out of hand. Apart from the vandalism of the moles, the turf was in wonderful condition for so early in the summer; and would become much finer still, in time for Mr Andrews to do what he does most years, scoop the prizes in the annual Beaulieu Horticultural Society competition. He is faintly bemused by the lack of interest shown by other society members in the matter of lawns. For him, it is simply an indispensable. He would no more live without a good lawn than he would have a house without a front door.

When Alan Andrews looks out of his window on to his little kingdom, he likes it to be as it should be. He admits, with a stifled noise midway between a laugh and cough, that he is distressed if something is amiss: a weed in a border, a shrub with brown-tinged leaves, a stalk of meadow grass on the lawn. He will not rest until the matter is dealt with. He likes his sharp edges, his straight lines, his neat borders, his well-ordered shrubs; and the forest beyond kept in its place, its anarchic licence at a safe distance. And I would surmise that nothing short of war, pestilence or irreversible infirmity would keep this decent and determined Englishman from his garden.

An Englishman of another type: Denis Burles, ex-RAF, late sixties, six foot three, bluff, business-like, perfectly friendly, but not the sort of chap you would dream of calling by his Christian name at first meeting. As befits a Lawn Doctor, he greets me with a corer in his hand: 'An invaluable tool,' he explains, for furnishing a cross-section of your turf. He lives with an unseen Mrs Burles on the outskirts of Abingdon, in a large house dating, I would guess, from the 1950s, surrounded by a large garden whose juxtaposition of lawn, border, gravel, shrubbery and mature trees is immediately and unmistakeably 'English' in its character, though I would be hard-pressed to explain exactly why or how.

He beseeched me not to look at his lawn, a most English species of diffidence, given that I had come on lawn business. It was, he said, not as he would wish it, for he had been too busy to get down to the necessary scarifying. Needless to say, it looked splendid, as flat as a tennis court (which was what it was laid down for), and glowing with health. Mr Burles is tremendously, insistently sensible about grass. He admires the usefulness of ryegrass, tolerates the odd patch of meadow grass, is indulgent towards daisies and clover, has nothing against moss in moderation, and reserves his hostility for plantains and their uncouth cousins. He has, in his work, seen and experienced the lawns of fantasy and perfection. He told me, in wonder, of the pure fescue lawn planted beside the Palumbo residence in Berkshire, bluish in tinge, soft as silk to the touch and rather more delicate, prodigiously demanding of care and the spending of money; an indulgence, he implied, for a plutocrat with a foreign-sounding name.

He is a judge of lawns and their owners, equating his work with political canvassing, of which he has done his share (for the true blue, I would hazard, but I would not dream of asking). He has learned, he says, to make judgements on his way to the front door, based on the situation and quality of the house, the care evidently given, or not, to the garden, the availability of light, the prevailing winds, the nature of the soil. The appearance and demeanour of the client completes the equation, and he knows where to start.

He has a quiet disdain for men who ask him, as if he were a plumber, to transform a paddock into a velvet sward in time for their daughter's wedding ten days hence; who inquire if he has heard of that 'magic grass' from Canada guaranteed to produce perfection in a trice. It is an article of faith with such a man that a decent

217

lawn cannot be, as it were, plucked from a shelf. To make it, there is a tried and tested combination of elements: soil made ready, seed of the proper kind, applications of fertilizer and weedkiller, and so on. Then there must be work, regular work: mowing, weed removal, scarifying, etc., etc. There should be nothing obsessive about this; it should be a 'working' lawn, for an Englishman to play English games like cricket, football, croquet, tennis, with his wife and family and friends he has known so long that it would take an effort to recall the circumstances in which he met them.

For such a man as Mr Burles, there are no easy ways, no shortcuts. Something worth having – a home, a wife, a business, a lawn – makes demands, otherwise it is not worth having. That is why Mr Burles mows two or three times a week (little and often, never cutting more than an eighth of the length of the grass, leaving the cuttings to lie to provide necessary food); why he was about to scarify when I saw him; why he submits himself to this regime of insistent demands on his time and energy, which Mrs Burles does not understand and rather resents (because he is rarely available to assist in the work of the borders and shrubberies), while naturally being rather proud of the result because of the way it sets off everything else.

It goes without saying that this lawn, being English, will accommodate immigrants benignly, as long as they behave themselves and follow the rules. Moss, clover, lower forms of grass life, are fine – as long as they know their place and keep it. But they must be restrained in their natural impulse to take over, to alter the essential character. And he is ruthless with what he terms the

'CBL' – common broadleaved weeds – such as plantains and dandelions. They are wholly anti-social types, spreading horizontally, breeding promiscuously, killing the grass beneath their wide fleshy leaves. They are poisoned without pity. But at the same time, he disapproves of fanaticism as much as licence. He has no time for those who seek to exterminate earthworms because their casts are unsightly, nor for the wasters of water with their emerald patches steaming in midsummer heat while the rivers run dry.

For a lawn in England to be a true lawn, it must have its stripes, light and dark; so Dennis Burles is, of necessity, a cylinder mower man. In his shed, among the sacks of fertilizer, weedkiller, pest controller and seed, stands the essential machinery: scarifier, hollow and solid tiner (for perforating compacted ground), rotary mower (for the rough stuff out of sight), push mower (for the little patches), and his prop and staff, an eight-blade Lloyds Paladin. Mr Burles is not one to wax sentimental about a machine, to call it 'she' and ascribe moods and characteristics to it. But it is clearly more to him than just a tool for a purpose. The relationship is perhaps akin to that between farmer and workhorse, permitting a brusque affection while sanctioning the knacker's yard. He cleans his Paladin and maintains it with care, because without that it would not work properly. But it would no more occur to him to prettify it, to restore the crimson of the cutters or the rich green of the bodywork than it would to the farmer to tie a pink ribbon in Dobbin's halter. To Dennis Burles the beauty of a machine and its usefulness are indivisible. The capacity of this mower to do the job better than anything else around, thirty or forty years after its manufacture, is the sole justification for its pride of place in his shed.

As I was leaving, he told me he was intending to cease practising as a lawn doctor. He was weary of the travelling, he said, and of the unreal demands of people with grass but no understanding of its ways. He wanted more time for his own garden. I speculated that what he had identified as a gap in the horticultural marketplace had proved to be much more demanding and less lucrative than he had hoped. I left him to his scarifying, pretty sure that he and his Paladin would be keeping each other company, master behind machine, keeping that decent bit of lawn in decent order, while there was strength in those long legs, and an edge to those burnished cutters.

I knew of Ransomes and Dennis, and something of Green, and Shanks, and Atco and the rest, among which Lloyds of Letchworth was but another name. But actually, when I thought about it, I knew a little more than that. I have a passion for fishing, and in my boyhood my hero had been Britain's pre-eminent angler, Richard Walker, who – when not stalking record carp, plotting the downfall of giant roach, or producing another instalment in an incomparably provocative stream of newspaper articles and books – worked as technical director for Lloyds. His mother, the legendary Mrs E. M. Walker (no first names, please) had joined the company as a clerk in her twenties when it was a mere importer of American equipment, and had risen to take control of it and direct it towards making lawn mowers instead of just dealing in them, remaining as chairman and managing director until she was nearly ninety. The Walkers, mother and brilliantly inventive son, are long gone. But the company survives and seems quietly to thrive, one of those unsung places where forty years of service is nothing exceptional; which stays small because that's the way they like it; where a fierce, silent pride in traditional notions of craftsmanship and good service means that their quiet claim to make the best lawn mower in the world cannot seriously be challenged.

You need to know nothing of the Paladin's high-carbon chromium steel blades, its spring-actuated plate clutches, its jockey wheel tensioner nor any of its other one hundred and one specifications to appreciate that it is a thoroughbred. There is nothing fancy or flashy about it; men paying £3,000 plus for a machine to cut the grass would not want that. It is sound, solid, splendid, not needing to pretend to be what it is not, being the best. You feel that Edwin Beard Budding, having recognized it as the child of his mind, would have thrilled with pride.

Denis Burles's was the first Paladin I had ever seen. The second was in James Rothery's garden shed, and it had on it not a blade of old grass, not the merest smear of earth. Mr Rothery told me, as if he were communicating the most mundane piece of information, that he washed it after each use – not cleaned it with an oily cloth and gave it a brush down, but washed it. I asked him how often he cut the grass. Oh, two or three times a week, he replied with a slightly unnerving smile. The rest of his equipment was in equally pristine condition.

It included an electric edger, the latest in its field and as quiet as a razor, and a Jacobsen Greens King ride-on mower, a new model of which retailed at around £18,000. I became aware that Mr Rothery's relationship with his grass was one of unusual intensity.

I had actually met him for the first time a couple of hours earlier, in what had been until recently the car park of the Wednesfield Conservative Club on the out-skirts of Wolverhampton. This area Mr Rothery and his workforce were transforming into a Crown Bowling green. I knew nothing about this sport. It was explained to me that it was played with keen competitive enthusi-asm by some three and a half thousand clubs spread over an area stretching from Carnforth in the north to Coventry in the south, and from Llandudno in the west almost to Huddersfield in the east. Like its southern cousin, flat-green bowls, it is played on the turf of the finest, smoothest quality man's ingenuity and labour can produce. Its distinguishing feature is that the centre of the green is raised a foot above the level of the periphery, providing a slope which the Crown Greeners stoutly maintain makes their game even more demanding of skill than the flat earth variety.

Mr Rothery had never, as far as I could tell, played either game, and certainly had no interest in them. What had engaged his attention – first as a diversion, latterly as a business – was the nature of the green itself. To make an area of anything between 660 and 1,000 square yards perfectly flat, and grow upon it perfect turf, are no easy matters. To engineer an expanse of grass with a minute, mathematically uniform slope from the centre requires a scientific mind of some distinction, which Mr

Rothery clearly has. As I have not, I could not really follow his exposition of the techniques involved, in which readings furnished by some sort of laser machine of his own devising played a central part. So I watched his men putting down the layer of blinding sand which, in the profile of the green, is sandwiched between the drainage stones and the upper root zone, the mixture of fine sand and loam which supports and sustains the cloth of the finest bents and fescues required for the bowls to roll true. The Wednesfield Conservative Club green was intended to be ready for use in the first year of the new millennium (actually they were playing on it by the end of the last season of the old one). It took little effort of the imagination to see the members in their ties and short-sleeved shirts and soft shoes and pressed trousers bending to their play, and hear the click of the balls and the murmurs of appreciation for this fine amenity.

Thirteen years before, Mr Rothery had, mainly by himself, constructed a rather larger green in front of his house in Cheshire. That is easily written, but the magnitude of the undertaking and the nature of the impulse to do it are hard to comprehend. The ostensible explanation – offered to me by Mr Rothery in a manner suggesting that he had no real expectation of it being believed – was that his wife loved bowling, and that this has been a gift to her. It was as if he had said that he had dug her a swimming pool by hand because she was a keen swimmer, or an Olympic-sized lagoon because she enjoyed sculling, or had created a replica of Epsom because she adored flat-racing. Mrs Rothery had never played on her personal bowling green for the very obvious reason that she was a member of a club with its own green, which competed in a league of clubs with their own greens.

So there it lies, a perfect square of improbably smooth, fine-leaved turf, spiritually isolated from the rest of the garden, like a private place of worship; a place where a single devotee pursues his rituals; a monument, not to its dedicatee, but the frankly admitted obsession of its creator with the stuff, grass. Mr Rothery is in no way ashamed of, nor embarrassed by, his passion, although he makes no real attempt to put it into words, and clearly expects himself to be regarded, on its account, as a little outside the normal. Asked about it, he says that he can remember, as a boy, clamouring to be allowed to mow. It just went on from that, he says, and he smiles as he admits – or boasts – that he can bore for Britain on the subject. Pressed, he searches for a touch of the romantic, a little beyond the technicalities, and comes up with something about the smell of cut grass.

On the day of my visit, he was in agony over the condition of the place of worship. Almost unceasing rain in spring had made it impossible for him to get on it to provide the pampering it needed to be anywhere near its best. He had not been able to scarify it properly, which meant that the vigour of spring growth had been inhibited by the profusion of thatch. Its colour was pallid, like the complexion of a child kept too long indoors. It wanted feeding and warm sunshine. Worst of all, to one side something had gone badly wrong with the system of pipes laid to drain excess water into the enclosing ditch. The ground was like a quaking bog, and had been invaded by rampant moss, which had discoloured it like some malignant disease.

Clearly discomfited by his ailing green, Mr Rothery took me to his shed. Stimulated by my admiration for his Paladin, he embarked upon a detailed account of how he had come by it, in succession to a Ransomes Auto Certies via a dalliance with an Atco Club so unsatisfactory that the managing director of Atco had issued a personal apology for the machine's shortcomings. I told him a little about Dennis Burles's philosophy of lawn tolerance, but Mr Rothery was thoroughly unimpressed. The notion that mowing should be done without the box, to allow the clippings to nitrogenize the turf, clearly struck him as doctrinally unsound. Earthworms and their casts he regarded as pernicious. When I asked him how he got rid of them, he smirked mysteriously and would say no more than 'I have my means'.

Around the house were arranged conventional lawns intersected by precise little paths enclosing borders and shrubberies. The divisions between sward – no nonsense about 'working lawns' here – and flower beds were as sharply defined as if they had been drawn with a fine nib. There were few flowers in the borders. 'Let's have a look at James's greenhouses,' Mr Rothery said, puzzlingly. Under the glass were serried ranks of bedding plants, their foliage and blossom beaded with droplets, their luxuriance moist testimony to the efficacy of the system of irrigation and temperature control refined by their proud owner. 'I'll be putting out four and a half thousand of them in a few weeks,' he said, as if they were toy soldiers.

As I left, he drew my attention to a minute patch of yellowing in the rich emerald of one of the lawns. 'Pearlwort,' he said ferociously. 'I've killed it.' He crouched.

'Look, here's another bit.' I looked, and identified a brushstroke of deeper green, a tangle of tiny leaves creeping around among the bents and fescues. 'I'll kill that next,' he said. 'I always have a knife in my pocket – you never know when you're going to come across a weed.'

Earlier, he had told me how the locals occasionally lobbed rocks and bits of metal over his high hedges on to his grass, presumably in the hope of disabling one of his machines. Mr Rothery attributed this urge to despoil to common envy for the superior being and his superior creation. But I wondered if it were not more akin to the destructive impulse of the Mongols of old, who, riding bareback out of the East, found towns and cities and razed them to the ground, because they did not understand the concept of a home.

If James Rothery might be seen as representing Puritanism in lawn cultivation, and Dennis Burles the broad church, then Bill Deedes is the prophet of the permissive tendency. 'I like my lawn uneven,' he says, regarding it indulgently. 'Why should I want a perfect lawn? I don't live in a stately home.' It's true, although once his family owned Saltwood Castle, on whose lawns the subsequent proprietor, the late Alan Clark, liked to be photographed mounted on a beast of a ride-on mower. Now, Lord Deedes's home is a stone-fronted Victorian farmhouse clad in creeper and climbing rose, with a path outside whose flags are worn and cracked and infiltrated by weeds; a solid, spacious, comfortable sort of a place for an elderly gentleman to return to from his wanderings, and warm his backside by the old Aga.

It lies on the edge of a Kentish village, where Erasmus once had the living, though the theologian's inability to speak a word of English inhibited his communion with his parishioners; and where a servant girl known as the Maid of Kent claimed to have had visions of the Virgin, until Cranmer forced her to recant and had her hanged at Tyburn. Very properly, Lord Deedes regards himself as a Kentishman, and is proud of it, although these days he is probably as familiar a figure in Albania or Sudan as he is on his home territory. At eighty-seven, he observes a discipline of work that would be considered taxing for one half his age, alternating between daily commuting to the *Daily Telegraph*'s offices in east London and hopping around the world's most horrendous troublespots, reporting on the agonies of the oppressed with unfailing compassion and insight. When I caught up with him, he was weekending at home for the first time in months, taking a brief breather at the height of the Kosovo horror, preparing for his imminent departure to the refugee camps of northern Albania. As he acknowledged without any sign of regret, the garden had to pay the price for his absence.

He gave me a cool, nutty beer from Kent's brewery, Shepherd Neame, and himself drank pink gins as he talked of the Kosovo war, forecasting (with impressive accuracy, as it turned out) that the Yugoslav capitulation would come within a few weeks. It was not easy to turn him from the subject of man's inhumanity to man to that of his grass. At length we went outside, and he showed me a paddock adjoining the garden, where the grass was supposed to kept down by a flock of fleeced foragers, except that they were not numerous enough or hungry enough to do the job properly. In his shed, a somewhat dilapidated structure, was assembled a collection of machines in a condition that would have given James Rothery nightmares, including a defunct Ransomes Marquis and a Toro recycling rotary mower clogged with old grass and decomposing leaves. He spotted the gardener escorting a beaten-up Honda rotary, and chided him for preferring such an unrefined creature.

Deedes himself properly scorns the circling blade. He is a cylinder man, his machine something called a Morrison, which is red, and which I had never heard of. (A few months after we met, he used his column to celebrate his reunion with the Ransomes, restored to life after an expensive visit to the repair shop.) When at home, he mows the best of the grass, between the house and a yew hedge, beyond which lies what used to be the vegetable garden, now laid to grass but some way short of graduation to lawn status. It takes him a couple of hours to do his share, the remainder being left to the foragers and the despised Honda. It is a good time for the mind, he says. The noise, the steady stride, the regular turning of the machine, bring up ideas for columns and speeches, and bring those half-formed to maturity. Even better is swinging the scythe, because of the quiet: 'You have a problem in business or private life,' he wrote in the *Telegraph* some years ago. 'Take out the scythe and the chances are that the answer will come to you.' The rare days he is around, he still swings the scythe, or strides behind his mower, or nurses his Bob Andrews Lawn Doctor as it devours the thatch, or fractures the peace of his thirty acres of woodland with the snarl of his chainsaw.

I asked him about the roles of men and women in the

garden. 'Women are planters and creators,' he replied, his old, parchment face creased in a smile. 'We like destroying things, and when we tell them about the splendid things we've destroyed, they're not in the least bit interested.' The gardener reappeared, and together they cooed and clucked over the yellow rose, climbing with cheerful vigour towards the first-floor windows, and discussed what Mrs Deedes (as her husband referred to her) might make of the tomatoes.

I became aware that my time was up, though my ancient host's civility would not have permitted him to say as much. He had a column to write for Monday, preparations to make for Albania next week, maybe Sudan in July. As I drove away, I recalled him describing how he had been sent by his newspaper to a school where the headmistress had wept as she described to him the poverty that had forced some of her girls to prostitute themselves. That had been in Lancashire, in 1937. I wondered how much grass he had cut in his time, how big the mountain of cuttings would be.

The Mowermen

The lawn is a living fossil in a modern human zoo
WALTER KENDRICK

T he two brothers, John C. Dennis and Herbert R. Dennis, began with bicycles in the 1890s, soon added motors to them, then expanded into the van and bus market. In 1924 Dennis Brothers of Guildford introduced their Motor Lawn Mower thus:

> The present is the Mechanical Age. Every labour-saving device is not only an individual economy, it makes for general efficiency. The self-propelled vehicle sweetens travel and cheapens transport; the self-propelled lawn mower makes grass-cutting a pleasure . . .

The words are suffused with confidence, and the brothers had made a machine to justify that confidence – not an adaptation of an existing mower with an engine bolted on, they hastened to add, but 'newly designed, from start to finish, as a complete unit'.

There were two models: the 24-inch, which cost £75, and the 30-inch, at £90. There was also a booklet, on whose cover was reproduced a masterpiece of commercial artwork, which is like a glimpse through a peephole into a forgotten world. It shows the ground-floor front-age of some broad-windowed country mansion. Between the windows are coils of luxuriant wisteria, beneath them beds bright with pink and white flowers. At the centre, the pillared entrance frames a trio of elegant upper-class ladies, in hats and slender skirts, as fragrant as the roses scenting the late morning air. Along the front of the house runs a wide gravel path, and beyond it a lawn enclosing a bed bursting with colour, with another path, running at right angles, and more lawn on its far side. The paths are as flawless as the complexion of the ladies, the edges as straight as rulers, and the grass is cut in stripes of complementary precision. In the foreground is the machine, a thoroughbred at rest, in burnished silver and glowing green, with the name Dennis inscribed in gold across the front of the box, the proud capitals framed in modest curlicues. Behind it, legs astride, hands gripping steel handles, is the mower man, in apron and sturdy shoes, wearing a tie but with shirtsleeves rolled up; not for a moment to be taken as having a blood tie with those scented society females, an unmistakeable member of the labouring class, but with a status defined by his relationship with the machine. His lordship may have signed the cheque, but this is the man's mower, its work his work.

The scene is powerfully pervaded with the flavour of its time. It is the England of late Galsworthy and early Agatha Christie, of eccentric lords and feckless sons, of coming out and the season, of bright young things and tennis parties; of the Drones Club and dressing for dinner, of ancient residences standing in ancient parks, built by the first Earl and maintained by retainers faithful to the fifteenth; an England still organized according to the principle of accident of birth, in which the right of those of the upper tier to enjoy themselves while everyone did the work remained pretty much unchallenged, except by a handful of socialists and other assorted troublemakers. It is an England which has been expunged. The lawns and borders and shrubberies are probably covered in 'executive-style homes' ; if they still exist, it will be because the mansion is now a hotel and conference centre. The descendants of the fragrant ladies will be in banking or stockbroking, those of the gardener in information technology, and the size of their mortgages will not be so very different. There will be one survivor. It is a fair bet that, somewhere, in the hands of some enthusiast for the Mechanical Age whose coming Dennis Brothers celebrated, that mower is still cutting stripes of light and shade.

The commercial drawback of the Dennis mower, Tony Hopwood explained to me, was that it was simply too well made. It may have been the Mechanical Age, but it was also the age of innocence, and the notion of planned obsolescence had not been invented. The design of the Dennis was, in its essentials, flawless, and it remained unchanged for the best part of fifty years. The quality of the materials and the construction meant that people who bought a Dennis did not need to come back to buy another. They merely had to send it periodically to the workshops at Guildford, from which – after attention at the hands of devoted craftsmen – it was dispatched literally as good as new. Over the years, the proportion of potential customers who became actual customers swelled, until there was hardly anyone left who might want a Dennis and did not have one; at which point the curtain came down on Dennis Brothers of Guildford.

Tony Hopwood is not a lawn man, which – in view of the fondness of badgers in his part of Worcestershire for pursuing worms through his turf – is as well. He could tell you nothing about the pedigree of his grass, has nothing against daisies and moss, and is wholly indulgent towards the badgers. The delight he takes in mowing his acre or so of lawn springs partly from the common desire to keep things neat, but, much more potently, from the opportunity it gives him to cement and celebrate, on a weekly basis, his bond with his machine. He is a mower man, a Dennis man.

He is also rather brainy. He has one of those angular, mobile faces behind which, you know at once, a good mind is at work. And he has clever hands to go with it. He trained as an engineer and ran an engineering business, but – after a late career change – now refers to himself as a geophysicist. His speciality is the sun, and the influence of its behaviour on climate. He was soon expounding to me his views on global warming, assuring me that its primary cause was not the excesses of the human race, but the activities of the great fiery ball in the sky; and that these would soon diminish in intensity, resulting within a few years in long, bitter winters with the snow lying deep.

From his office came the chugging of a battery of devices monitoring assorted solar phenomena, which were churning forth charts decorated with spiky readings of the comings and goings of ultraviolet and cosmic rays, heavy particles, electric fields and the like. Elsewhere, surfaces were littered with a host of ancient radios and their parts, while shelves sagged under the weight of scientific treatises and obscure histories inspired by the development of telecommunication. Outside, in the middle of the lawn, was a contraption of strange aspect, which Mr Hopwood said he had invented to measure flare activity around the sun. He tried to describe how it worked, but I could not begin to follow him; and, anyway, I was anxious to make the acquaintance of his Dennis.

It and his other mowers were berthed in a brick and beamed barn built by Mr Hopwood on the other side of the chocolate box cottage. First, he pulled out a Ransomes Mark Seven of 1933; 'an engineering cock-up', he called it fondly, on account of the misplacing of the gravitational centre which meant that, left to its own devices, it tipped over backwards. There were other machines in the shadows, an Atco mower of the thirties, an oil-powered Crossley mill engine salvaged in Rochdale, a Myford lathe beneath the window.

But my eyes were for the Dennis. Mr Hopwood smiled with an almost paternal pride as he produced the child which had been fourteen years old when he was born. It bore the number 5155, and had been rolled out of those Guildford workshops in 1926 – the year of the General Strike, the deaths of Houdini and Rudolph Valentino, of England's first Ashes win over Australia since before the Great War. Unlike the Dennis my father had bought twenty-odd years later, this had the flat-topped petrol tank (I preferred the curved, Mr Hopwood the flat – we Dennis men are like that). Otherwise every feature was familiar to me, from the gleaming levers standing vertical at the back to the pregnant swell of the grass box at the front. And the scraping and grinding of the back roller as Mr Hopwood dragged it out into delicious early May sunshine were the same, as evocative as a tune once tinkled out on the nursery piano and heard again.

Mr Hopwood itemized its attributes – the 500 cc Blackburn engine, the cone clutches, the aluminium gear case, the hardened steel faces and soft centres of the cutters. He had but one cavil about the design, the awkward protrusion of the magneto. But what was that, weighed in the balance against the magnificent efficiency of the engine, and the brilliant concept of supporting the grass box on arms acting as pivots, which enabled the contents to be tipped out with an easy swing, rather than laboriously lifted. Mr Hopwood shook his brainy head in admiration. The Ransomes, the Atco, the Webb – nothing could compete with the glory of the Dennis. 'It is', he said, glowing with affection, 'the king of mowers.'

But would it perform? Even the sturdiest septuagenarian can be fallible, and he was clearly nervous. The first two turns of the starter handle produced nothing more animated than a raspy cough. But at the third, the life came flooding in. There was a deep, deep roar. Half a ton of metal throbbed and pulsed. Mr Hopwood smiled in relief and pleasure, hopped on to the curved metal seat at the back, rumbled across the gravel to the grass, thrust forward the inner of the two levers to join the outer. Grass speckled with daisies leaped forward, like a wave on to the beach.

Would I like a go, he shouted above the clamour? Of course – I must, it was what I had come for, a sentimental journey into the past. I knew there could be no reliving the experience. For that, I would have needed our lawn, free from flare-tracking machine, various decrepit apple trees and old stumps and the trenches left by the badgers, and our Dennis, seatless, in its slightly deeper green livery, and rounded petrol tank. But there was enough in my two circuits of Mr Hopwood's lawn to taste the flavour of long ago: in the crunch as I engaged the cutters, the throaty crescendo as I depressed the accelerator, the whirr of the cutters, the spray of the grass; enough to make me meet Mr Hopwood's smile of delight with a grin appropriate to that spotty, gangly, clumsy, gloomily virginal schoolboy of long ago.

He had found the Dennis on a scrap yard in Tring thirty years before. It had previously been the property of the Thames Valley Constabulary, and he had paid £15 for it. To bring it back to working order began as an exercise in exploring the possible, and became a labour of love. He spent countless hours with it in his workshop, repairing and replacing the defective parts. And when he had finished resurrecting this masterwork of engineering, he went out and found another victim of abuse and neglect – Denise, he called the invalid sister, with a suitably embarrassed laugh – and started all over again.

Tony Hopwood was in the grip of a self-confessed passion for the workings of what he persisted in referring to as the 'internal confusion engine'. To him, unlike me, these were not mysteries, but aspects of a beautiful harmony, which – in the hands of those nameless craftsmen of Guildford – had reached its highest peak of achievement. He had nothing but contempt for the trumpeted technological advances of our own day; 'Mickey Mouse stuff', he called it. He was sure that the brother and sister – when she was back on her rollers – would outlive him. A Dennis, unlike its owner, had been built to last.

It is somehow characteristic of our age that, even as we have severed ourselves from our traditions of manufacturing excellence, so should we have developed a taste for wallowing in nostalgic tenderness for its artefacts. In the not so dim past, the notion of a rusting assemblage of old metal occupying useful space in the garage having an intrinsic worth, even beauty, would have been considered absurd. Brainwashed into embracing the new, people threw out the old, whether or not it still functioned usefully. Then they found that the new – however beguiling its image and ingenious its design – fell to bits before it had performed a tiny fraction of the service of its predecessor. And they became sentimental about the passing of an age in which machines had been made, not by other machines programmed by computers, but by craftsmen, to last.

In time that pining for times past came to embrace the humble lawn mower. Once, old mowers could be found – like Tony Hopwood's Dennis – in junk yards, on the scrap heap, in skips, at dumps. Not even the least pretentious of country auctions would take them, though you might fall over one thrust into an unconsidered corner at the local jumble sale. But gradually –

as the large-scale manufacture of top-class cylinder mowers was becoming another part of history – the nostalgic passion asserted itself.

A man – always a man – who had, over the years, almost unwittingly, accumulated a few old mowers in his shed and had fallen into the habit of tinkering with them at odd moments, would find himself one day at the sale in the village hall; where, as he crouched beside some rust-ravaged Atco or battered Ransomes, he would become aware of someone else regarding the machine with the same air of informed admiration. And they would get talking, swapping tales of a Shanks salvaged from the tip, a JP Simplex found in the mother-in-law's shed, a Webb Witch snapped up at the cricket club's annual sale. And one would ask the other if he had ever bumped into so-and-so, who had a Dennis in perfect order and maybe a Samuelson, or an early Qualcast; and if he hadn't, he soon would. Thus a brotherhood was born.

There was an innocence about this species of collecting. The obscurity and cheapness of the desired object was part of it. To the pleasure of the hunt and the kill was added that of discovering the affinity with other hunters. Suddenly an association was born, of kindred spirits who could never have come together in the normal course of work or family life. Thus, ten years or so ago, the Old Lawnmower Club was born.

In collecting, the age of innocence lasts as long as supply comfortably outstrips demand. There comes a time when the awareness of a hitherto unsuspected appetite permeates the second-hand market. The collectors find that the old sources are becoming barren, that the channels of supply have come under the control of professionals alert to the fact that desire to possess translates into willingness to pay. Innocence and the profit motive cannot co-exist; and the fragile flower of innocence is the one trampled on. It happened ten or fifteen years ago with old fishing tackle. Within a short period, the admiration of the few for the elegance and durability of equipment made to assist in the catching of fish spawned a hot, selfish lust for ownership. Amateur collectors turned into professional dealers, laymen were elbowed out, tackle buffs who had once pooled knowledge now kept secrets; and soon the London sale houses were holding auctions of fishing tackle at which men with sharp faces arranged matters among themselves while the rest of us goggled and gasped at the prices.

The Old Lawnmower Club began as a loose association of like-minded enthusiasts, but has become much more than that. It has around 250 members (of whom one is female). It organizes rallies and shows and outings, negotiates with museums, takes itself quite seriously. Its energetic and assiduous secretary, Keith Wotton, produces a neat and lively magazine called *Grassbox*, which dispenses information and pronounces on the issues of the day. Of these, none is more pressing, nor more indicative of the shedding of innocence, than that dealt with in a recent editorial under the headline: 'Where have all the mowers gone?'

The obvious answer is that most of the mowers of yesteryear were scrapped when their owners had no more use for them. Some, that shrinking residue of such burning interest to the members of the Old Lawnmower Club, are still lying around waiting to be snapped up. A small number are in museums. The rest are in the hands of collectors, most of whom are like Mr Hopwood, with a handful of cherished models. But there are a few who, because their appetites were keener and their circumstances more congenial, have accumulated on a grander scale. Among these, two stand out: two cousins, Andrew Hall and Michael Duck, who – having independently and coincidentally been bitten by the bug – separately and later together have pursued the passion with an unrivalled energy, persistence and cunning. The fruits, known as the Hall Duck Collection, are contained in a warehouse in Somerset: somewhere between 700 and 800 offshoots in the vast family tree which has the original Ferrabee Budding at its head.

I assume that Andrew Hall is the senior in the partnership. He is a man of Sheffield, and is concerned that he should not be taken for anything else, given to lingering over his vowels in a manner designed to repel any soft southern notion of cultural oneness. Behind his gleaming forehead and its spectacles is a repository of knowledge about lawn mowers vaster still than the hoard which bears his name. He is a man who glories in his learning. A favourite prelude to an Andrew Hall pronouncement is: 'What you've got to understand is . . .', after which he will exhume some detail from the history of the side-wheel mower manufactured in a corner of Milwaukee around 1888 or so, and present it to you with the air of someone who has just found a missing piece of a jigsaw down the back of the sofa. Mr Hall will not permit himself to be bested in the knowledge stakes. Whatever anyone else knows about mowers, he knows. Whatever they do not know, he does. Whichever mower they may have, he will have one, too; usually better, earlier, rarer, more authentic.

There is a story to each heap of old metalwork in the Hall Duck Collection, and he loves to tell them. Many begin as tales of good fortune: how some ancient treasure was glimpsed among nettles in a backyard, or half-buried in a skip. But they swiftly metamorphose into accounts of the hunter's perspicacity, historical awareness, ingenuity and determination. The conclusion is invariable – the trophy is added to the Hall Duck Collection. I never heard of the one which got away.

The first time I met Mr Hall he was preparing for a trip to America, to organize the shipment back to the Collection of an assortment of prizes which he had managed to pluck from beneath the noses of American collectors. The next time I saw him, he told me about one of these coups. It concerned a tiny Thomas one-wheel edge-trimmer – 1883, in original order, naturally – which he had spotted tucked away in an antiques shop in Massachusetts. The climax to the narrative came – not with the amazement of his companion when shown the discovery, boundless though that was – but in the settling of the account with the female assistant. The machine cost thirty-seven dollars, and was exempt from some tax or other because it was for export. The assistant asked how she should know it was going abroad. 'Do you know what I said?' Mr Hall said to me, with the air of a conjuror.

'No.'

'I said, "Listen to the accent, LUV." ' He beamed triumphantly.

That second meeting took place at a steam fair in Oxfordshire, where a small sample from the Hall Duck

Collection was on display, together with the proprietors. Most of the machines were American – 'to impress our Yank friends', Andrew Hall explained. He conducted me through the distinguishing features of the 1938 Locke, with its floating cutting cylinder, and of the 6-inch Caldwell from the 1890s, and of the early 20th Century Imperial, and of the red and gold Townsend Victory. At last he was distracted by some other seeker after knowledge, and I was able to speak to Michael Duck. I asked him about their 1895 Shanks pony mower, which has featured prominently in the duo's occasional television appearances. He responded with a well-rehearsed and detailed account of its discovery in a barn near South Molton in Devon, and subsequent rehabilitation. 'What about this?' I asked, pointing to a Follows and Bate 10-inch Climax.

'I tell you,' said Duck with a Wessex chuckle, 'I bloody near 'ad a climax when I got that.'

The ensuing narrative was complex, involving a boot sale, several rounds of negotiation in the pub, a visit to a man in the woods and the handing over of a hundred quid. A similarly tortuous chain of events preceded the acquisition of the 1855 Samuelson Budding, an exceedingly rare treasure first spotted in a pile of scrap. ' "Fuckinell," I zed when I zaw it,' recounted Duck with a grin. 'When I showed it to Andrew, 'ee zed, "Fooking 'ell." '

The man of Sheffield reappeared and started telling me how they had secured a 1912 30-inch water-cooled Ransomes from an Irishman whom they had originally contacted with a view to laying their hands on a Shanks pony mower. The story had many twists and turns before arriving at its finishing post. 'How much did you pay for it?' I asked.

'Am I going to tell you that?' Mr Hall demanded theatrically. 'Not bloody likely.'

The Hall Duck Collection is an epic tribute to the zeal and passion of two men, far superior in scale and range to anything in a museum, and all the more remarkable for the massive archive of documentation which supports it. But it is deficient in one important respect. Both Andrew Hall and Michael Duck – and, for that matter, every other lawn mower collector in the land – have a dream. It is to find, acquire, possess an original Budding. In lawn mower terms, this would be the equivalent to obtaining a violin carved and strung by Stradivari himself, a First Folio signed by Shakespeare, a copy of Bede's *History* with corrections in the Venerable One's own hand. The mystery, thus far unsolved, is whether such a thing exists at all. Ransomes, in Ipswich, have a very early machine which – according to oral tradition – was made by them to the original Budding patent. The fact that it has the secondary roller behind the cutting cylinder proves that it pre-dates a Ferrabee Budding in Stroud Museum, which has the roller in front. Another very early machine – also with the roller behind the cutters – was presented to the Science Museum in 1928 at the request of a Lady Owen McKenzie. But it, too, came from Ipswich. Of an original Budding actually made at Ferrabee's factory at Thrupp, no trace has yet been found.

Andrew Hall told me that he believed there was at least one such machine extant. My inquiry as to its possible whereabouts and provenance stimulated a lip-smacking, head-shaking, eye-bulging display of incredulity at my naivety. I asked Michael Duck if he thought such a thing existed. 'Well, I met this bloke, 'ee zed how much would you pay for a Budding and I zed how much would you want and 'ee zed mebbe four or five hundred quid and I zed well, let's see it first, then we'll talk about money. I dunno, mebbe 'ee 'as got one.' He shrugged his shoulders, eyes bright with hope.

With all this talk of the mowers of the past, I began to feel a sharp nag of regret at the passing of our Dennis, and a feeling of dissatisfaction with my current machine. For many years, on a variety of pretty unrefined lawns, I had been content with what is a thoroughly decent, dependable, workhorse of a mower; able to chew up and spit out the thickest of rough grass, cowslips, nettles and brambles; to shrug off encounters with sticks and stones which would incapacitate more delicate machines; and yet also able to lay down a passable finish on a respectable lawn. I have never given it, my Hayter Harrier, a tithe of the care I should have, and it has repaid me with thirteen years of unstinting service, and the promise of many more to come. But, as the seeded patches of my new lawn began to show green and call for cutting, I yearned for something better. The Hayter is a rotary mower, and my fine-leaved grass cried out for something more suited to its refined ways. Only a cylinder mower would do.

Here budgetary constraints intruded in their unpleasant way. My heart longed for a glistening new Lloyds Paladin (at around £3,500) or a valiant Dennis of yesteryear. But I had neither the surface area to justify such an outlay, nor the wherewithal to accomplish it.

Then I had a stroke of good fortune. I went to see a man called Michael Hardy, a retired zoology lecturer, who – according to Andrew Hall – was a canny collector of old mowing machines. Beneath his silver hair, set in a genial face, Mr Hardy's eyes had a softly acquisitive gleam to them. He was a haunter of junk shops and auction rooms and car boot sales, an unabashed gatherer and hoarder of the flotsam of the past. The state of his shed and his garage testified to the keenness of his enthusiasm, and the energy with which he pursued it. He collected antique secateurs, old watering cans, ancient fishing tackle and books on angling, binoculars, magnifying glasses. And then there were his mowers, stacked up on top of each other, the mound inhibited from collapse by an intricate web of rope. There was a Shanks, various Ransomes, an Atco, a crop of JPs.

These machines, made by Jarrow and Pearson of Leicester between the 1920s and the 1960s, were Mr Hardy's particular joy. He pulled out his Super Simplex, purred over the baffling complexities of the clutch system, the curve of the burnished aluminium petrol tank, the meanderings of the slender pipe leading from it, the extravagance of the brass fittings, the elegance of the wooden-sided grass box; then poked a couple of times at the carburettor, pulled the starter rope, and sent it away amid a plume of blue smoke.

Later, he complained that he had an excess of mowers, and muttered something about being amenable to disposing of one or two. I had had a soft spot for the JP since coming across an old advertisement for a Super, showing it standing gracefully on a sun-drenched lawn beside a voluptuous Aphrodite under the caption

'Masterpieces'. But it became apparent that Mr Hardy was far from weary with his JPs. He was, however, prepared to part with another small part of British mowing history – if not a masterpiece, still, in its modest way, a classic.

Ransomes introduced their Ajax series in 1933. By 1948 the Mark Three – 'ideal for keeping any small lawn in trim' – was selling in its thousands. The Mark Four came in the late 1950s, its combination of 'strength with lightness', according to the advertisement, making it the ideal companion for a firm-breasted, laughing blonde in calf-length patterned summer dress. By 1964, though, masculinity had reasserted itself. A Brylcreemed salesman in a brown suit is inviting a solid citizen in hat and blue serge, with a pipe clamped in firm, square jaw, to part with twelve pounds fourteen shillings and sixpence to obtain the Mark Five: a 'lightweight, quality-built and attractively styled roller mower for the well-kept lawn'. A brief turn on Michael Hardy's grass was enough to persuade me that we – the Ajax and myself – were made for each other.

Gleeful, I took it home, and found that the passing of forty years since its manufacture had done nothing to diminish the qualities suggested by its warrior lineage. A steady thrust set the steel cutters turning with a low, purposeful whirr and the tender, juicy cuttings flew forward. It was like a schoolmaster of the old sort, a tweed-jacketed no-nonsense sort of mower, stamping its authority firmly but fairly through its stripes. All it required was a dry place to rest, the occasional squirt of oil and wipe with a dirty rag, the periodic tightening or loosening of a nut here and there. I found it much more restful to use than the clamorous Hayter; nor, being a push mower, did it have the annoying habit of running out of petrol when the mowing was 95 per cent done. I relished the modest physical effort it required of me, and the marvellous efficiency of its design. My Ransomes Ajax was, quite simply, a joy to use.

FOLLOWS & BATE

The
" CLIMAX "
8-in. 50/-
10-in. 63/-

My Sward and Others

Consider the many special delights a lawn affords: soft mattress for creeping baby; worm hatchery for a robin; croquet or badminton court; baseball diamond; restful green perspectives leading the eye to a background of flower border, shrubs or hedge . . . as changing and spellbinding as the waves of the sea, whether flecked with sunlight under trees of light foliage, or deep, dark, solid shade, moving slowly as the tide

KATHARINE S. WHITE

Romantic aspiration inspired my sowing. Had I followed the dictates of dreary common sense, I would have used what the Doctor defines as Utility Lawn Grass seed, since I was treating ground next to existing areas of mediocre turf which I could not be bothered to nurse to excellence. The principal constituent of this mixture is perennial ryegrass, *Lolium perenne*, a plant of several sound virtues. It is properly green, grows energetically, is tolerant of drought and does not wilt away from periodic neglect. It is the stuff, as the Doctor persists in saying, for football and cricket and the pounding feet of children. But it is not the stuff of romance. Glamour and style it does not have. It is the grassy equivalent of kitchen units of pre-fabricated melamine and crushed woodchip.

It is undeniably useful, but its stalkiness and the coarseness of its leaves disqualify it from the vision of the velvet sward.

In the families of grasses, ryegrass keeps company with a variety of associates – some serviceable, some harmless, one or two downright objectionable. Chief among the last category is annual meadow grass, *Poa annua*, which cannot find a place in the most debased mixture sold by the seed merchant and avenges itself by blowing in uninvited on the wind and setting up home where it is not wanted. Smooth-stalked meadow grass, *Poa pratensis*, on the other hand, has always been and remains socially acceptable: neat in appearance, reasonably well-mannered, valued for its willingness to establish its roots in shady places. It is to be preferred to its rustic cousins, *Poa trivialis* and *Poa nemoralis*, and stands in terms of respectability beside that old favourite of Mrs Loudon and Shirley Hibberd, crested dog's tail, *Cynosurus cristatus*.

But I was like Becky Sharpe, unable to content myself with the commonplace. I craved for higher things, the Doctor's Luxury Grade Lawn, a sweep of even, uniform turf, dense with soft but vigorous fine-leaved grasses, aglow with greenness and a quiet sense of its own high standing. Even as I craved, I knew that it could never happen, unless I dug the whole thing up, levelled it properly and started again; a labour from which I recoiled. My compromise was to introduce the higher ideals on the new patches, to establish an example of refinement in the hope of persuading the strongholds of daisies and clover and the clumps of rough meadow grass to forsake their uncultured ways.

I inquired a little into the ways of the gentrified grasses.

I found that some spread by dispatching little stems underground, which are called rhizomes, the habit of the plant being therefore defined as rhizomatous. Others creep around overground, by means of stolons, and are therefore stoloniferous. Others merely form tufts, and – if the place is suitable – more tufts. There are two great dynasties among the fine-leaved grasses, the bents (*Agrostis*) and the fescues (*Festuca*). Like all large families, they have their high achievers, their plodders and their wastrels, and it has taken a considerable expenditure of scientific effort to establish which combinations of which members are of most value to the lawnsman. Sheep's fescue, for instance – *Festuca ovina* – was popular in Mrs Loudon's day, but it has a solitary tendency, is excessively fond of forming hummocks and finds it difficult to exist in peace with other grasses. Velvet bent, *Agrostis canina canina*, is comely enough but handicapped by the shallowness of its roots, which causes it to flag in times of drought.

The acknowledged champion among the *Festuca* family is Chewing's Fescue; for which we have to thank a Mr Chewing, about whom nothing much seems to be known beyond that he purchased some grassland in the Waimea Plains of New Zealand in the 1830s on which sprouted a herbage of such exceptional quality that someone eventually had the idea of collecting its seed and sending it to the Old Country to make lawns. Chewing's Fescue is both blue-blooded and a worker: non-rhizomatous, rooting intra- and extra-vaginally, dense, tufted, with a slightly bristly tubular leaf, commendably drought-resistant, tolerant of most soils, and – most important – a good team player, able to get on with other grasses. If it has a weakness, it lies in its placid nature. It can get crowded out by other, more aggressive grasses.

Its favoured partner among the members of the *Agrostis* dynasty was also first developed in New Zealand. Browntop bent was exported from the Waipu district, whence – according to those who have delved into the by-ways of grass history – it had been brought from Prince Edward Island in the 1850s. It is both rhizomatous and slightly stoloniferous, tough but classy, easy-going, another good team player. It does, however, take time to establish itself; while, concealed in its genetic constitution, is a proclivity to dominate. It is therefore normally restricted to no more than a fifth of the mixture. It is nursed by the quicker-growing fescue, and then, as time goes on, it tends to take over.

After the tedious labour of weed and stone removal, raking, stamping and the rest of it, the sowing of the seed came as a welcome diversion. Not that the Doctor would have it so. His recommended programme of action demands the raking of furrows, the division of the seed into four equal parts to be distributed in four directions, more raking, and the arrangement of a tapestry of criss-crossed black thread above the seed bed to discourage the birds from eating the stuff. But by now I found myself becoming a touch rebellious under the weight of the orthodoxy. I ran my fingers through the mixture of fine fescues and browntop. It was dry and rustled pleasantly. Then I cast it upon the ground wherever my steps took me, until the brown of the earth was nicely flecked by the pale needles, and the box was empty. I sieved a smattering of soil and compost on to the seed, firmed it down, and left it.

I had actually done the front lawn some time before, and had realized after a while – during which nothing happened – that I had jumped the gun, and that the soil had not warmed sufficiently to quicken my seed into life. By the time I resumed operations, summer had tiptoed in. There were soft breezes from the south, occasional periods of benign sunshine, and a good deal of the best sort of rain – not pounding downpours, but soft and drenching.

Germination is a wondrous thing. There comes a morning when you are, as you do most mornings, staring forth from an upstairs window at your bare patches, reflecting, as you invariably do, on the baffling way in which the stones which you have removed by the barrowful are replaced from mysterious sources by other stones, when you realize that the patch is not bare at all, that it has been brushed with colour, as if a green mist were clinging to it. You hurtle forth, and there, magically appeared among the stones, are the first little drifts of the risen grass, blades cobweb thin, hardly strong enough to be looked at, let alone touched.

Yet they are amazingly energetic in their growth, these tiny pins of green. Each day the tinge strengthens, suggestion becomes reality. It is still a fragile thing, but it has declared itself as here to stay. You may now tread upon it carefully, stoop to pluck out the nasty sprigs of weed which have shot up in competition, perhaps even venture a light roll with the mower tilted back, to encourage rhizomes and stolons to do their stuff. Hovering in your mind is the thought of the first mow, the coming of age.

*

Those moments have something of the unalloyed joy and excitement of attending the birth of a child; and, like childbirth, are followed by much tedious care. Would that making and having a lawn were merely a matter of watching the grass grow, and then marching up and down on it in the sunshine making neat patterns on it, and laying the harvest on the compost heap. The matter of weeds spoils all that.

I know that there cannot be gardening without weeds. They are like midges, motorway cones and jar tops which cannot be unscrewed – pinpricks of nuisance which the mature person learns to manage with a smile and a shrug of resignation. Nor am I a racial purist where my lawn is concerned. I am prepared to put up with daisies and clover in moderation, would not wish to exterminate pearlwort, will turn a blind eye to a minor sprouting of mouse-ear. But there are some invaders whose habits put them beyond the pale. I will not stand aside and permit the odious ribwort and other plantains to have their way. Nourished by their deep, pale taproots, they spread their fat, fleshy leaves along the surface and, if left to their own horrible devices, send forth their flower heads atop ridiculous waving stalks, seeking to cast their spawn on the wind and extend their territory. The notion of team play, live and let live, is abhorrent to them. Their sole instinct is conquest.

Those conditions of warmth and damp which had helped the infant grass on its way were equally delightful to the plantains. While my attention was occupied elsewhere, they multiplied. If I had been on top of the situation, I should have resorted at once to chemical attack and sprayed them with some disabling poison. That is

what the Doctor would have done. But I had vague inclinations towards the organic floating in my head, the
thought that perhaps there might be a third way, between
excessive permissiveness and Stalinist oppression. By the
time I became fully aware of the menace, it was too late
for liberal compromise. Armed with hand fork, a narrow
trowel, a chisel and a screwdriver, I waged war on my
knees, prizing out my enemies one by one. I removed
five large bucketfuls of casualties, until my fingers were
stained tobacco yellow with their bitter juices, the lawn
was defaced with spots of bare earth and my heart was
filled with detestation for these useless creations.

The most fervent wildflower lover would be hard pressed
to find beauty in plantain or ribwort. But there is music
and poetry in other lawn-loving flowers: bird's-foot trefoil, mouse-ear hawkweed, speedwell, hawkbit, selfheal,
woodrush, dove's-foot cranesbill, storksbill, madder,
cinquefoil, crowfoot and celandine. To the Doctor,
naturally, they are all enemies, plants growing in the
wrong place, to be assaulted with a double or triple action
killer. Since the development of the first chemical weed-
killers, this has been the prevailing orthodoxy. It has at
its heart the assumption of a conflict between grass and
this host of adversaries, in which Man – with his management control programme and armoury of weapons –
must constantly intervene if his grass is not to be over-
whelmed.

Some years ago the Duke and Duchess of Devonshire
were advised that intervention on an epic scale was necessary to rescue from the paths of unrighteousness the two

lawns which grace the east side of Chatsworth, providing the foreground to Paxton's fabulous cascade. They are known as the Salisburys, and are, very likely, the oldest authentic lawns in the country. They were laid in the 1760s on the instructions of Capability Brown, and replaced the terraces of parterres and fountains which had delighted the first Duke. Brown, ruthless as ever in his disdain for the past, had the ground smoothed and harrowed and levelled and sown with hayseed. It was then left to itself for a couple of centuries, being grazed by deer into the 19th century, and thereafter mown by a succession of horse- and petrol-powered machines. It was never sown with any reputable grass seed, nor treated with any fertilizer, nor raked nor scarified. Nor did any-one bother about the vast diversity of plant species which found discreet sanctuary with the grass; until the 1980s, when it was noticed that the Salisburys did not look much like a normal lawn at all. The turf priests at the Bingley Research Institute near Bradford were consulted. They prescribed chemical attack, to be followed by recoloniz-ation with socially acceptable species of grass. At this point a Doctor Gilbert of Sheffield University leaped forward to advise the Devonshires that, in approving Bingley's strategy of racial purification, they would be consigning a living tableau of gardening history to the dustbin. It is much to the Duke and Duchess's credit that, notwithstanding their deep disapproval of Capa-bility Brown's original act of destruction, they ordered a reprieve for the Salisburys.

Doctor Gilbert and the head gardener at the time, Mr Hopkins, set about classifying the elements comprising this extraordinary heterogeneous carpet of herbage.

Apart from most of the inoffensive flowers mentioned above, and a medley of mosses and lichens, they found heathers, violas, harebell, tormentil, sweet-vernal grass, yarrow, ox-eyed daisy, ladies bedstraw, sorrel and cat's ear. This gorgeous, species-rich tapestry has ever since been allowed to proceed on its own sweet way, assisted by the occasional spiking to restrain the moss from running rampant, and a weekly mow. Viewed from the cascade, the sward seems almost to lap at the feet of the golden walls of the great house. Its surface is like that of a shifting sea, jade merging into emerald, light into dark, alive with secrets and changing moods. It is a marvellous, indispensable place for the lover of lawns to linger. Its diversity and capacity to surprise lift a curtain on the possibilities of your own lawn. And as you leave Chatsworth, you may stop where the bridge crosses the winding Derwent, and watch – as I did – the trout snaffling early mayflies; and look back at the house, luminous in early summer sunshine, and away across the park, at the wedges of woodland deployed by Capability on the skyline to the west, answered by the hanging woods on the eastern escarpment, with the great sweeps of pasture being cropped, as in days of old, by the fleeced forager.

I returned from Chatsworth inspired by a new tolerance and appreciation of the multi-ethnic lawn; which was as well, in view of the flourishing condition of the mouse-ear, clover, daisies and their friends. The new grass was also gaining ground. It looked at its best at first light, when the pallor of the green was brushed with the silver of the dew clinging to a tracery of minute cobwebs. By day it became apparent that the overall colour scheme was rather more distinctly variegated than that at Chatsworth. The green of the new grass was markedly more pale than that of the old, a contrast which struck me as either rather interesting or wholly absurd. The splashes of white provided by the clover, the yellow wink of the rogue buttercup, the stardust of the daisies and the different greens of their foliages, all added their tones.

I decided to make a virtue of the price I was paying for not adhering properly to the Doctor's teaching. Having already expended the equivalent of a working month on weeding, stoning, raking, stamping, sowing, sieving and the rest of it – not to mention of a small fortune on soil, compost and seed – I simply could not be bothered to initiate an attritional war against the weeds. I told myself that there was no need to see my lawn as a test of my will and my manhood, that I had matured from that. To be sure, the Salisburys were two hundred years old and more, and mine but two months; and what could be regarded in Derbyshire as a gloriously rich integration of species might well appear at the rear of 27 Wood Lane as the symptoms of gross neglect. But, I reminded myself, there were more important things in life than the state of the garden, and more important things in the garden than the lawn, and more important things about the lawn than persecuting unwelcome intruders.

I went to Stowe in Buckinghamshire to ask the head groundsman, Steve Curley, about the task of keeping two hundred acres of high-grade turf in order. He took me to his shed, which was as big as an aircraft hangar and needed to be. He had eight men working under him, and an arsenal of machinery at his disposal, including five Ransomes Certies and a Lloyds Paladin for the close-cutting work, a Ransomes Mastiff 36-incher, a Jacobsen and a Beaver; and ranks of assorted lesser mowers, leaf blowers, edgers, strimmers, line painting machines, spray guns, fertilizer spreaders and much else besides. With six cricket squares, a golf course, assorted tennis courts and decorative lawns to be maintained, borders to be weeded, hedges to be trimmed, shrubberies to be spruced up; with Speech Day looming and everyone from the headmaster down reminding him – as if he needed reminding – of the importance of the place looking its best, Mr Curley was working most of the hours permitted by the rotation of the planet and was in no mood to consider a policy of appeasement towards his traditional foes. Grass was there to be cut, weeds to be killed, pests to be poisoned, worms to be harried and harassed, moles to be gassed.

Nor, as he hurried from one chore to the next, did Mr Curley have much inclination to pause and savour the atmosphere which is still so strong about this extra-ordinary place. So I left him to his dark reflections about Speech Day and wandered off, in search of the spirits of Cobham, Kent, Bridgeman, Brown and the others whose imaginations and ambitions and talents had come together to transform this valley into a place of infinite delight. I strolled past the Queen's Temple and Concorde, in the shade of great sycamores and wellingtonias, and skirted the Grecian Valley, where the long grass, spangled with buttercups, bent with the breeze. I took the path past the Temple of Worthies, paying my respects to Milton, Locke, poisonous Pope and their companions, and breathed in an air rich with the damp of age-old mulch and water weed. I came to the Octagonal Lake, with the Palladian bridge to my left across a grassy slope being nibbled intently by fleeced foragers. Tadpoles swarmed at the water's edge and lily pads stirred in response to secret motions below.

I moved along the bank, until I could stand with the lake behind me and look up towards the long, low south face of the house, its pale golden stone glowing in the sunshine. I found the glory bequeathed by Cobham intact, and it required no great effort of the imagination to surrender to it. But just as surely has it been diminished in our time. The necessity of maintaining Stowe as a school has spawned a notable assortment of inappropriate and downright nasty contemporary buildings, most of them mercifully hidden away in the trees. And what, one is compelled to wonder, would that distinguished soldier and patron of the arts have made of the squads of golfers in their peaked caps and canary yellow polo shirts, trundling their trolleys through his landscape of classical and literary allusion, whacking their little white balls in the direction of the drawing room Vanburgh had built him?

Weaving my way between the foursomes, I made my way up to the house, to look out from the top of the semi-circular flight of stone steps leading down from the south portico, and drink in the wonder of the composition. Is there anything finer in the gallery of garden landscape than this panorama? It is bound by the distant hillside, where the horseshoe of the Corinthian Arch stands. In the middleground is Bridgeman's lake, guarded by a brace of pavilions whose reflections dance on the open water between the beds of lilies. The fore-

259

ground is framed by dense woods of beech and chestnut, studded with the darker green of ancient yews and cedars. Almost from your feet, stretching down to the water, is the most superb sweep of turf imaginable: a lawn neither flat nor uniform in its slope, nor perfectly manicured, with its share of weeds and patches of wind-blown coarse grass, but incomparable in the way its emerald richness completes a great work of art. Its grandness, among the follies, absurdities and singular flights of fancy and genius, helps give Stowe its nobility. It must have filled Cobham's heart with pride; apprehending, as perhaps he did, that the art of shaping Man's inheritance to his pleasure could hardly reach higher.

At first sight, the Great Lawn at St John's College, Oxford, would appear to exemplify the hoary dictum that the route to perfection in a sward is to lay the grass on a flat surface and to mow it regularly for two or three hundred years. Actually it does nothing of the sort, for, two centuries after the gardens were created by Capability Brown, the drought of 1976 killed off almost all of it. The magnificent turf that stretches away from the hydrangeas beneath the windows of Archbishop Laud's library is less than a quarter of a century old, and is the product of a rigorously observed programme of care which is entirely dependent on contemporary machinery and chemicals. It is scarified, hoovered, solid-tined, hollow-tined, autumn fed, spring fed, rolled, weeded and mown and mown and mown.

When the second gardener, Barry Bowerman, came to St John's the best part of forty years ago, almost all this labour was done by hand. The moss and thatch were taken out by wire rakes, the weeds removed one by one, the spiking done by fork, the ten tons of leaf mould required for the autumn top dressing sieved two spade-fuls at a time. Times have changed – the size of the gardening staff has diminished, and so have their hours; new accommodation blocks stand where peaches, nectar-ines, grapes and vegetables were grown to feed the dons and their students; and the standard of care for the Great Lawn has been lowered, as the donkey work has been taken over by machines. But the principles of feed-and-weed, roll-and-mow are still observed. And the results – I was slightly troubled to find – are a ringing endorse-ment of the disciplinarian approach.

The lawn at St John's is 180 yards long, 100 wide, and to mow it with the rotary Hayter, as Barry Bowerman periodically does, involves a seven-and-a-half-mile walk. It is enclosed at one end by the south side of the second quadrangle, and on the others by tall and stately copper beeches, chestnuts, oaks and sycamores, interspersed with shrubs and beds. The effect is dual. There is a gran-deur about the scale, which is as generous as a city setting could reasonably permit; but with it comes that atmos-phere of seclusion, intimacy and reflective tranquillity which those antique seats of learning still retain and make available to those prepared to take a few steps from the street past the porter's lodge. Stand on the gravel path before the Great Lawn of St John's, let the eyes play over the rich carpet of verdure – forgetting that it owes its condition to several hundredweight of nitrogenous fertilizer, and not to any special quality in the air – and one can feel, with Henry James, that the college garden is a refuge 'from the restless outer world . . . a place to lie down on the grass forever, in the happy faith that life is all a vast old English garden, and time an endless summer afternoon'.

I came back from St John's resolved that the Chatsworth creed of tolerance could be taken too far, that without some degree of discipline there was a danger of anarchy and social disintegration. On my front lawn the mouse-ear was out of control, driving what was left of the grass into headlong retreat. At the back the contest was in the balance, but the ranks of the weeds were reinforcing themselves, while my fescues and bents were on the back foot. With a tremor of remorse, I filled a watering can thrice with Verdone weedkiller, and did the dirty deed.

There was another serious upset. A small patch of the grass which I had sown on what had previously been a wild and woolly thicket of rose and other plants suddenly withered. Its perishing was accompanied by a mysterious elevation and cracking of the surface. It looked like a cold sore, and through the cracks were pushing little clumps of green leaves. I removed the dead turf and dug down. As I lifted the soil I uncovered quantities of revoltingly misshapen tubers resembling pieces of fresh ginger, from which had burst fat, penis-like shoots reaching upwards. They were, my wife told me, the remnants of a plant called a fatsia, the removal of whose subterranean support system had evidently been incomplete. The fatsia joined the sumach on my list of arch-foes.

I tried not to give way to retributive gloom about the

perfection of other lawns; to stand back from the petty disappointments and irritations, and recall the wilderness that our garden had been a few short months before. Just as at Stowe, the best view of our garden was from the house. True, ours was obtained from the back door or the kitchen window, rather than a pillared portico; and we had neither Corinthian nor Doric Arch, but a pseudo-rustic affair from the timber yard down the road; and our answer to Kent's Temple of Ancient Beauty was a rectangular shed of creosote-stained wood and rusty corrugated metal. But there were other affinities. Like Cobham and his men, Helen and I were seeking – albeit on a more modest scale – to impose upon disorder a concept of harmony. And by the end of that summer, as the beds she had planted bloomed, and the rose and clematis crept around the trellis and up towards the rustic arch, and the grass laid root, and the old apple and hazel trees bore their fruit, and the conkers on the chestnut swelled, we had no great difficulty in persuading ourselves that we had given a new lease of life to the place.

In retrospect, I can identify the application of that weedkiller as a watershed in my personal history as a lawnsman. The moment I emptied the sachet into the watering can and turned on the tap, stirring the powder and inhaling the smell of death from the frothy, greyish liquid, I took a decisive step back into the camp of conformity. We went away for a week at the end of September, to Corsica (where there are no lawns). When I came back, I found that the killer had begun its work.

The mouse-ear, the ribwort, the plantains, were looking far from cheery. Their upper leaves were twisted and curled, those lower down yellowed and rotted by the poison. I took away a couple of bucketfuls of victims, which left the sward looking decidedly poxed. I decided that, having gone thus far, I must go forward again.

The approved programme of autumn lawn care has two major features: scarification and the application of a top dressing. The purpose of scarification is to remove dead grass and other accumulated rubbish, allowing the stems of the grass light and air, which are good for them. It may be done with a wire rake, deployed – in the Doctor's words – with 'considerable downward pressure'. Having done a good deal of this wearisome work earlier in the year, I had no desire to do any more. So I went to the local hire shop and asked if they had a machine to do it for me. I was presented with a motorized cylinder bristling with a fearsome array of slicing edges, arranged to savage the turf when revolved at speed. Fired into life, it roared and bucked in my hands, tearing at the surface like a wild animal. Within an hour, what had previously at least resembled a lawn was mutilated into something else.

By the end of the next day I had spread across my poor, wounded lawns a healing dressing of mixed topsoil and laboriously sieved manure. This extremely tedious procedure is defined by the Doctor as 'vital' for the achievement of first-rate turf. But I fear that in omitting some of the detail – adding sand and peat to the mixture, the use of something called a lute for distributing it, and the filling in and levelling of holes and hummocks – I may have mitigated the overall effectiveness. I was also a month later than I should have been, and the weather had settled into that state of permanent melancholic moistness typical of late October. As a consequence my dressing, instead of being dry and friable and willing to be brushed into the roots of the grass, tended to settle in damp lumps, which would attach themselves to the soles of my gumboots as I tramped to and fro. Apart from making my feet absurdly heavy, reducing me to an astronaut's lumbering tread, this produced new declivities where the lumps were missing, making the expanse more uneven than ever.

But I pressed on. The final part of the operation was the belated reseeding of the grassless patches. To avoid collecting mobile seed-beds beneath my boots, I went barefoot, skipping with wet, white feet across the sodden surface, scattering seed as I went, and hoping very much that no one could see me.

Since then I have done nothing to the lawn – except walk on it, look at it and think about it. To be frank, its condition is terrible. The grass, what is left, is lank and feeble. Where a few months ago it sprang resiliently to the upright position when trodden upon, now it lays down in surrender. Its green is not vital but sickly. There are worm casts everywhere, dark curls of slimy earth extruded from wormish bottoms and rendered into slippery smears wherever anyone has walked. I am beginning to wonder if tolerance of worms cannot be taken too far.

It is the evening of December 4th, a Thursday. The sun has shone all day from a sky of the palest eggshell blue, but without any warmth to lift the dampness which has settled like a sodden blanket on the outside world. The leaves lie dank and heavy, the branches of trees are slippery with the wet. The earth is dark and secret. Walking down to the bonfire, I seemed to feel the ground quaking beneath my feet. The tread of my boots produced a muted squelching sound, and left prints in the mud on the grass.

I wonder how I could ever have been so absurd as to think that I could create a greensward. Nevertheless, this morning I did something I have never done before. I took both the mowers from the shed, the Ransomes Ajax first, then the Hayter Harrier. I scraped the muck from the cutters and rollers and massaged them with an oily rag. I cleaned the dark crannies of their accumulations of dead matter, squirted oil into nipples, junctions and holes. For the first time in history, I managed to find the implement for removing the spark plug from the Hayter, which I decarboned with a wire brush and returned. Like a groom with favourite horses, I took my time, pausing now and then to admire the fine lines and robust build of my charges. Finally, I rubbed linseed oil into the wooden front roller of the Ajax. It was not obligatory, the manual said, but advisable to prevent cracking. I felt it was a gesture of commitment, perhaps even of penitence for past neglect.

It is dark now and the mowers are back in the shed, side by side, clean, sleek with oil, conspicuously cared for. I confess to feeling virtuous, having done my bit for them, repaid them, as it were. The grass still rebukes me though, for my pride and my carelessness and my dereliction. But I am consoled, because spring and summer will make all that right. I can see it now: the turf thick, smooth, springy, glowing in its green glory, offering itself up to the whirring motion of well-lubricated cutters. It is very forgiving stuff, grass.

BIBLIOGRAPHY

Bacon, Francis, *Essays, or Counsels Civill and Morall*, 1612.
Batey, Mavis, *The Historic Gardens of Oxford and Cambridge*, 1989
Baker, C. H. C. and M. I., *The Life of James Brydges, Duke of Chandos*, 1949.
Beale, Reginald, *The Book of the Lawn*, 1931.
Blomfield, R. and Thomas, F. Inigo, *The Formal Garden in England*, 1892.
Borman, H. and others, *Redesigning the American Lawn*, 1993.
Cobbett, William, *The English Gardener*, 1833.
Comito, Terry, *The Idea of the Garden in the Renaissance*, 1978.
Daniels, Stevie, *The Wild Lawn Handbook*, 1995.
Downing, Andrew Jackson, *Rural Essays*, 1853.
Evans, R. D. C., *Bowling Greens*, 1988.
Evelyn, John, *Kalendarium Hortense*.
Fiennes, Celia, *The Journeys of Celia Fiennes*, 1947.
Fish, Marjery, *We Made a Garden*, 1956.
Godfrey, Walter, *Gardens in the Making*, 1914.
Hadfield, Miles, *A History of British Gardening*, 1969.
Halford, David, *Old Lawnmowers*, 1982.
Harvey, John, *Medieval Gardens*, 1981.
Hibberd, James Shirley, *The Amateur's Flower Garden*, 1878.
——, *The Town Garden*, 1859.
Hill, Thomas, *The Profitable Art of Gardening*, 1563.
Hyams, Edward, *Capability Brown and Humphry Repton*, 1971.
Jackson, Kenneth T., *The Crabgrass Frontier*, 1985.
Jacques, David, *Georgian Gardens*, 1983.
James, John, *The Theory and Practice of Gardening*, 1728.
Kemp, Edward, *How to Lay Out a Small Garden*, 1850.
Knight, Richard Payne, *The Landscape*, 1795.
Landsberg, Sylvia, *The Medieval Garden*, 1995.

Lees-Milne, James, *The Earls of Creation*, 1962.

Loudon, John Claudius, *Encyclopaedia of Gardening*, 1822.

——, *The Suburban Gardener and Villa Companion*, 1838.

Loudon, Jane, *The Ladies Companion to the Flower Garden*, 1846.

M'Intosh, Charles, *The Practical Gardener*, 1828.

McLean, Teresa, *Medieval English Gardens*, 1981.

Macky, John, *A Journey Through England*, 1714.

Mahnke, Frank H., *Colour, Environment and Human Response*, 1996.

Mason, William, *The English Garden*, 1783.

Markham, Gervase, Cheap and Good Husbandry, 1614.

Miller, Philip, *The Gardener's Kalendar*, 1757.

Partridge, Michael, *Farm Tools Through the Ages*, 1973.

Pollan, Michael, *Second Nature*, 1991.

Price, Uvedale, *Essays in the Picturesque*, 1794.

Rea, John, *Flora – A Complete Florilege*, 1676.

Repton, Humphry, *An Inquiry into the Changes of Taste in Landscape Gardening*, 1806.

Robinson, William, *The English Flower Garden*, 1883.

——, *The Wild Garden*, 1894.

Sanecki, Kay, *Old Garden Tools*, 1979.

Scott, Frank Jessup, *The Art of Beautifying Suburban Home Grounds*, 1870.

Scott-Jenkins, Virginia, *The Lawn – History of an American Obsession*, 1994.

Shenstone, *Unconnected Thoughts on Gardening*, 1764.

Sitwell, Sir George, *On the Making of Gardens*, 1909.

Switzer, Stephen, *The Nobleman, Gentleman, and Gardener's Recreation*, 1715.

Tann, Jennifer, *Gloucestershire Woollen Mills*, 1967.

Taylor, Geoffrey, *Some 19th Century Gardeners*, 1951.

Teyssot, Georges (ed.), *The American Lawn*, 1999.

Thacker, Christopher, *The Genius of Gardening*.

Tresemer, David, *The Book of the Scythe*, 1981.

Walpole, Horace, *On Modern Gardening*, 1780.

Waters, Michael, *The Garden in Victorian Literature*, 1988.

Wright, W. (ed.), *Practical Gardening for Pleasure and Profit* .

INDEX

Abingdon 216
Academy of Armory (Holme) 35
Addison, Joseph 22, 54, 60, 69
Albertus Magnus 15, 23, 24, 33
All-England Croquet Club 128
Alton Towers 84
Amateur's Flower Garden, The (Hibberd) 135, 137
André, Edouard 144
Andrews, Alan 213–16
Anglo-Saxons 17, 18
Angus, William 72, 73
Anna Karenina (Tolstoy) 42
Archimedean 128, 129–30, 136, 144
Ardsley, New York 160
Argyle, Prof. Michael 202
aristocrats 72–4, 77, 120, 133, 154, 175
Arlington 161–2
Arnold, Matthew 83
Art of Beautifying Suburban Home Grounds, The (Scott) 154
Art of Gardening (Worlidge) 40
Ashridge 74
Asterix 197–8
Atco 178, 183, 186, 225, 234

Bacon, Francis 36
Barber, Samuel 81
Bartholomew De Glanville 24, 25

Bate, John 130
Beale, Reginald 178–81
Beaulieu 214–15
Beloff, Prof. Halla 202–4
Benedictines 19–21
Better Homes and Gardens 163
Bingley Research Institute 181, 255
Birkenhead Park 138
Black and Decker 186
Blomfield, Reginald 173
Boccaccio, Giovanni 26
Bogo de Clare 16
Book of the Lawn, The (Beale) 178–9
Books of Hours 28
Bormann, Herbert 167
botany 45, 121, 182
Bowerman, Barry 261
bowling greens 23, 34, 39, 43, 44, 45, 48, 64, 149, 223–4 crown 222–3
Brasenose College, Oxford 44
Brentwood Golf Club, Long Island 161
Bridgeman, Charles 55, 56, 61
Brimscombe Mill 104–5, 114
Brithnod, Abbot 16
Broughton, Rhoda 140
Brown, Capability 61–2, 64, 68–71, 72, 73, 74, 255, 256, 260
Buckingham Palace 145

Budding, Edwin Beard
    107–13, 115, 117, 118,
    131, 221
Burke, Edmund 62
Burles, Dennis 216–19, 225
Burlington, Lord 54, 56

Cadbury Brothers 146
Cambridge colleges 44
camomile lawns 35
Canons, Middlesex 46, 50, 56
Carnegie, Lindsey 124
Carson, Rachel 167–8
Castle Howard 55
Celts 18
Central Park, New York 153
Challis, Thomas 129
Chambers, Sir William 68–9
Chandos, Duke of 45–6, 50,
    56
Charles II 39, 40
Chatsworth 64, 133, 255–6
Chaucer, Geoffrey 26, 27
Chewing, Mr 250
Chiswick 56–7
Chiswick Gardens 127
Christchurch, Oxford 44
Clairvaux 22
Claremont 55
Clarendon 23
Clarissa Harlowe (Richardson)
    66–7
Clark, Alan 226
classicism 55, 56–7
cloister garth 21, 24
clover 65, 136, 150, 156, 178,
    218
Cobbett, William 25, 120,
    135, 150
Cobham, Lord 61, 259, 260
Cocke, Gen. Hartwell 149
Coldwell Lawn Mower 159
Columbia mower 144
Complete Amateur Gardener, The
    (Thomas) 178

Conaty, Mr 128
Conway Castle 23
cottage gardens 143
Crabgrass Frontier, The
    (Jackson) 150
Crace, Jim 205–6
cricket grounds 95–6, 146
Crowley Invincible mower 144
crown bowling 222
Crystal Palace 143
Curley, Steve 257–8
Curtis, Mr 116
Curwen, Mr 82

Dahlman, Karl 184
D'Argenville, Antoine Joseph
    Dezallier 32, 47
Davis, Alexander Jackson 152
Davis, William 107
DDT 165, 168
De Vegetabilis (Albertus
    Magnus) 23
Deane lawnmower 127–8
Decameron (Boccaccio) 26
Deedes, Lord (Bill) 226–8
Dennis Brothers 91–7, 178,
    186, 230–7, 244
Devonshire, Duke and
    Duchess of 254–5
Dickens, Charles 150
Doctor Cupid (Broughton)
    140–2
Downing, Andrew Jackson
    151–2
Drake, Sir Francis 35
Drayton Green 84
Duck, Michael 240, 242–4
Durdans 44
Dursley 111012

Eden, Garden of 15
Edward IV 34
Edward VII 145
Edwardian age 172, 175, 177
Egyptians 41

Eleanor of Castile 23
Elizabethan age 32, 35–6
Elvaston Castle 133
Ely 16, 18
Elyot, Thomas 25
Elysium Britannicum (Evelyn) 43
Empson, William 83
'English Garden, The' (Mason) 62
English Gardener, The (Cobbett) 25, 120
English Husbandman, The (Markham) 33
environmentalism 168–9, 170–1
Epsom 44
'Essay on Modern Gardening' (Walpole) 61
Essays (Bacon) 36–8
Essays on the Picturesque (Price) 69
Evelyn, John 41, 43, 68

Ferrabee, James 124–8, 130–2
  Budding 108–20, 123, 125, 127–8, 240, 243
  Improved Mowing Machine 113–14, 126
  Noiseless Lawn Mower 126
Ferrabee, John 106–9, 111, 113, 115, 116, 118, 131
Field, John 45
Fiennes, Celia 44
Fish, Marjery 188
Fish, Robert 138
Fitzgerald, F. Scott 158
Flint, Charles 156
Flora (Rea) 41
Floure and the Leafe, The 26
Flymo 184–5, 186
Follows, Frederick 130
Fontainebleau 39
Formal Garden in England, The (Blomfield) 173

France 39–40, 47–8, 53
Freedom Lawn 168, 170
Frome, River 101, 104, 111

games, lawn 90, 218
Garden in Victorian Literature, The (Waters) 140
Garden Kalendar, The (Miller) 25
Gardener's Chronicle 112, 126–9, 142, 182
Gardener's Magazine 75, 109, 116–17, 118, 134, 138
gardening 29, 32, 77, 81, 120–1, 123, 126, 133, 176–7, 186–7, 189–90
Gardening Club of America 161, 162
Gardens in the Making (Godfrey) 173
gender 123, 164–5, 197–206, 228–9
geometric gardens 40, 54, 61
Georgian age 53–4, 75, 120
Gibb, James 63
Gilbert, Dr 2555
Gilpin, Revd William 67, 69, 79
'Glory of the Garden, The' (Kipling) 174–5
Godfrey, Walter 173
Golden Valley 101–5, 107
golf 160–1
Grace, W.G. 146
Granada 28
Grand Tour 55
Grasmere 81
Grassbox 239
grasses 136, 152, 156, 166, 191–2, 248–51
Great Exhibition (1851) 111, 125
Great Gatsby, The (Fitzgerald) 158–9
Great War 175–7, 180

green, symbolism of 22, 23
Green, Thomas, & Son 125,
    127–8, 129, 130, 183,
    186
  Silens Messor 125, 132
  steam-powered mower 145

Hadfield, Miles 29, 32, 46
ha-has 59, 61, 62, 73, 149
Hall, Andrew 240–3, 245
Hall Duck Collection 240–3
Hamilton, Charles 65–8
Hamilton, William 149
Hardy, Michael 245–6
Hardy, Thomas 83
Hartley, David 22
Hartley & Sugden Balmoral
    144
Hartwell House, Bucks 63–4
Harvey, John 24
Hayter rotary mower 244, 261,
    266
Hearne, Thomas 44
Henderson & Sons 137
Hennesy *Book of Hours* 28
Henry II 23
Henry III 23
Henry IV 34
Henry VII 29
Henry VIII 34
Hessayon, Dr David 49, 58,
    190–4, 209, 248, 251,
    264
Hibberd, James Shirley 134–7,
    178, 181, 209, 249
Hill, Thomas 32–3
Hirst Charm 144
History of British Gardening
    (Hadfield) 29
Holme, Randle 35
Holt & Willis Easy 144
Honda 186, 228
Hopkins, Mr 255
Hopwood, Tony 232–7, 240
House Beautiful 162

How to Lay Out a Small Garden
    (Kemp) 138
Hudson, W.H. 172
Hugh of Fouilloy 22

Industrial Revolution 74, 104

Jackson, Kenneth T. 150
Jacobean age 34, 35–6
James, Henry 133, 140, 175,
    262
James, John 47–52, 57, 58,
    61, 173, 190
Jefferson, Thomas 67–8,
    149–50
Jekyll, Gertrude 182
Johnson, Dr Samuel 25,
    59–60
JP Engineering 178, 186,
    245–6

Kalendarium Hortense (Evelyn)
    41
Kemp, Edward 138
Kent, William 55, 56–7, 61
Kenwood 84
Kew Gardens 69, 125
Kinnaird, Lord 124
Kipling, Rudyard 174–5
Knight, Richard Payne 69, 134

labour 80, 86, 174–5, 177
Lady of the Unicorn tapestry 28
Lake District 81–2
lakes 64, 67, 73
Lamson-Scribner, F. 156, 158,
    161, 166, 173
'Landscape, The' (Knight) 69
landscape gardening 56, 61,
    62, 73
Lane Fox, Robin 142–3
Langley, Batty 57–9
Lasseter Fairy 145
lawn:
    creation of 23, 33–4, 41,

49, 64–5, 152, 173,
179, 210–13, 248–52
definition 25
first 23, 27
lawn care 58, 79–80, 86,
187–8, 192–4
beating 41, 50
mowing 3–12, 93–6, 122,
123, 136, 143, 155,
167, 180–1, 197, 198,
202–4
rolling 41, 50, 63, 83
scarification 264
scything 41–3, 63, 73,
79–80, 110, 120, 129,
147, 152, 228
sweeping 79–80
tools 41, 43, 164, 219
top dressing 264–5
watering 192
lawn care industry 164–8,
170, 182
Lawn Institute 170, 171
lawn mowers 6–9, 91–3,
95–6, 230–47
American 128, 129–30,
144, 156
collecting 237–45
cylinder 110, 125–6, 131
design advances 124,
125–6, 129–30, 144–5,
177, 183–6
electric 184–5
hover 184–5
industry 124–31, 144,
177–8, 183, 186
petrol-driven 145–6, 177–8
pony-mower 124–5, 128,
141, 242
prototype 108–15
rotary 183–4
screw 129–30
steam-powered 145, 146
see also under individual
makers

Lawrence, Mrs 84–6
Leasowes, The 59
Lee, Sir Thomas 63
Legend of Good Women
(Chaucer) 26
Le Nôtre, André 39, 40, 47
Levitt, William 163
Levittown, Long Island 163
Lewis, John and Joseph 105,
107
Leyland Steam Motor
Company 145
Life Magazine 167
Lindley, John 126
Lister, George 112
literature 26–7, 42, 139–42,
158–9
see also poetry
Llewellyn Park 152–3
Lloyds of Letchworth 220–1
Paladin 186, 219, 221, 225,
244, 258
Lockner, Stefan 28
London County Cricket Club
146
Lorris, Guillaume de 27
Loudon, Jane 75, 123, 134,
136, 249
Loudon, John Claudius 72,
75–81, 84–6, 116–17,
121–3, 134
Louis XIV 39, 40
Luxborough, Lady 59

Madonna in the Rose Arbour
(Lockner) 28
Mansfield, Earl of 84
Markham, Gervase 33–4, 37
Marvell, Andrew 42–3
Mason, Revd William 62, 64,
69, 134
Merrick, A. 109, 118
middle ages 16–17, 26–30, 34
middle classes 74–7, 120, 121,
133, 163

Mills, Charles B. 163–4, 170
Mollet, André 39
monasteries 18–23, 31
Mongredieu, A. 137
Monticello 68, 149
Moor Park 44
morality 60, 75, 76, 117, 122,
    134, 148, 149, 151, 153,
    155, 156, 158, 163, 169
moss 136, 178, 200, 209–10,
    218
mounds 37, 44
Mount Vernon 149
Mumstead Wood 182

Napoleon III 125
Nature 54, 58, 60, 60, 121,
    143, 152, 199, 206
Nebot, Balthasar 63
New College, Oxford 44
New Lawn Expert, The
    (Hessayon) 191
New Principles of Gardening
    (Langley) 57
New York Times 169
Newton, Sir Isaac 44
*Nobleman, Gentleman, and
    Gardener's Recreation, The*
    (Switzer) 57
Norman Conquest 18, 29

Observations on Man (Hartley)
    22
*Observations on Several Parts of
    England* (Gilpin) 69
'Of Gardens' (Bacon) 36–8
Old Lawnmower Club 238–9
Olmsted, Frederick Law 153
Oxford colleges 44, 260–2

Painshill 65–8
painting 26, 28, 63–4, 70
Palladio, Andrea 57
Palumbo family 217
Paradise Lost (Milton) 25

parterres 46, 48, 58, 63, 74
Paxton, Joseph 126, 133, 138,
    142, 143, 255
Pembroke College, Oxford 44
Pepys, Samuel 39, 143
pests 165, 168, 178, 179–80,
    193, 200–1
Pettigrew, Mr 127
*Philosophical Inquiry into…the
    Sublime and the Beautiful*
    (Burke) 62
Phoenix Ironworks 106, 107,
    113–15, 125, 127
Picksley, Sims Imperial 144
picturesque movement 67, 69,
    74, 79, 82
Pinckney, Mrs 149
Pinturicchio 28
pleasure gardens 23, 24, 28,
    139
Pliny 17
poetry 26, 42–3, 55–6, 62,
    82–3
Pollan, Michael 148, 169
Pope, Alexander 54, 55–6, 68,
    133
Port Lympne 182
Portrait of a Lady, The (James)
    140
*Practical Gardening for Pleasure
    and Profit* (ed. Wright) 176
Prestcott Westcar, Mr 146
Price, Revd R. 129
Price, Sir Uvedale 69–70, 82,
    134
Pugh, Charles H. 178

Qualcast 178, 183, 185, 186

Radcliffe, Mr 129
Randall, H.A. 106
Ransome, Arthur 160
Ransome, James 145, 146
Ransomes 126, 130, 131, 183,
    186, 228, 234

Ajax 246–7, 266
Automaton 130, 131
Budding 113, 119, 124, 243
Certies 96, 258
Little Gem 130
Mastiff 258
motor mowers 145, 177
Rea, John 41
Redisigning the American Lawn (Bormann) 168
Regent's Park 125
Repton, Humphrey 70, 73–4
Richard II 34
Richardson, Samuel 66
Richmond Palace 55
Riverside, Chicago 153
Robinson, William 143
Rohde, Eleanor Sinclair 147
'Rolling the Lawn' (Empson) 83
Roman de la Rose (de Lorris) 27, 29
Romans 17–18, 42
Rothery, James 221–6
'Rural Essays' (Downing) 152
Russell family 45
Rydal Mount 82

Sackville-West family 182
St Albans 37
St Gall 21
St James's Park 39
St John's College, Oxford 260–2
Samuelson & Co 125, 127, 242, 267
Sapperton 103
Sassoon, Sir Philip 182
Schery, Robert W. 170
Science Museum 243
scientific research 155–6, 157, 160, 161–2, 166, 181
Scott, Frank Jessup 153, 154–5, 170

Scott, O.M., & Sons 161, 163–4
Seats of the Nobility (Angus) 72
Seats of the Nobility and Gentry (Watts) 72
Second Nature (Pollan) 169
Second World War 162, 182
seed 49, 58, 65, 135, 136, 150, 159, 161–2, 173, 251
Shaftesbury, Earl of 84
Shakespeare, William 25
Shanks, Alexander, & Sons 124–5, 127–30, 136, 183, 186
motor mowers 145, 178
pony mower 242
Shay Rotoscythe 183–4
sheds 5–6, 201
Shenstone, William 59–60, 66
Shread, John C. 168
Silent Spring (Carson) 168
Sissinghurst 182
Small House at Allington, The (Trollope) 139–40
Spectator 54
Spergula (spurry) 137
statuary 45, 46, 58, 63, 64, 84
Stevens, Mrs 44
Stowe 61, 257–60
Stroud 102, 107, 243
Stuart age 44
Suburban Gardener and Villa Companion (Loudon) 76
suburbia 77, 133, 138, 146, 150–5, 163, 172, 174
Suffolk Punch mower 183
Sumner, James 145
Supplee Hardware Co. 144
Switzer, Stephen 57–9

Taylor, Frederick Winslow 166
Taylor, Samuel 118
Tempest, The (Shakespeare) 25
Temple, Sir William 34, 44

temples 54, 55, 56–7, 63, 67, 77, 84
Thames-Severn canal 102, 103, 104
Theory and Practice of Gardening, The (James) 46–52
Thomas, H.H. 178
Thrupp Mill 106–7, 108, 111, 243
Tolstoy, Leo 42
topiary 45, 54, 58, 63, 64
Town Gardener, The (Hibberd) 135, 137
town gardens 135
Tradescant, John 45
Trentham 133
Trinity College, Cambridge 44
Trollope, Anthony 139
Truman, Harry 162
Tudor age 31, 32
Tuileries 39
turf 41, 49, 120, 135, 159, 166
turfing tools 41, 43
Twickenham 55–6

Unconnected Thoughts on Gardening (Shenstone) 60
United States 68
  golf clubs 160–1
  lawns 148–71, 181
  mowers 128, 129–30, 144, 156, 183, 242
  turfgrass industry 164–8, 170
US Congress 157
US Department of Agriculture 156, 160, 161
US Golf Association 160, 161

Vanbrugh, Sir John 55
Vaux, Calvert 153
Victoria, Queen 132, 133, 146

Victorian age 75, 121, 124, 142–3, 146, 172
Villa Palmieri 26
Virginia, University of 150

Waite, Burnell & Huggins Excelsior 144
Walker, Mrs E.M. 220–1
Walker, Richard 220–1
walks:
  gravel 33, 34, 37, 38–9, 40, 44–5
  turf 34, 44, 173
Waller, George, & Sons 114
Walpole, Horace 57, 61, 68, 133
Washington, George 149
Waters, Michael 140
Watts, William 72, 73
We Made a Garden (Fish) 188
Webb 186
Wednesfield Conservative Club 222–3
weeds 165, 179, 192–3, 200, 219, 225–6, 253–4, 262, 264
Westminster, Palace of 23
Whately, Thomas 134
White, Katharine S. 248
White House 169–70
wild flowers 191, 254–6
Wilde, Oscar 53
William and Mary 45
Wilton House 129
Windermere 82
Windsor Castle 23
Woburn 44, 45
Wood & Sons 125
Wooton, Sir Henry 38
Wordsworth, Dorothy 82
Wordsworth, Mary 81
Wordsworth, William 81–2, 84
Worlidge, John 40, 41
Wotton, Keith 239
Wright, W. 176–7

278

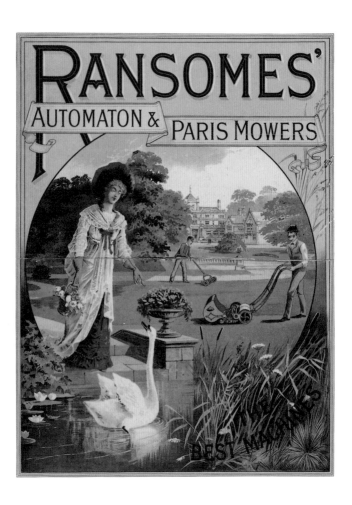

RANSOMES'

AUTOMATON & PARIS MOWERS

THE BEST MACHINES